UPON A DAY

Verse and Other Writings

GORDON GETTY

Copyright © 2024 Rork Music.

All Rights Reserved. This book contains material protected under International and Federal Copyright Laws and Treaties. Any unauthorized reprint or use of this material is prohibited. No part of this book may be reproduced or transmitted in any form or by any means, electronic or mechanical, including photocopying, recording, or by any information storage and retrieval system without express written permission from the author/publisher.

ISBN: 979-8-88636-042-4

BISAC CODES:
POE000000 Poetry/General
POE005010 Poetry/American/General
MUS028000 MUSIC / Genres & Styles / Opera

CONTENTS

INTRODUCTION BY THE AUTHOR.................................. 1
VERSE FROM COLLEGE AND BACHELOR DAYS 3
   My Uncle's House.. 4
   George Lewis.. 5
   Sonnet 6
   On T.S. Eliot... 6
   Two Elegies 7
   St. Christopher 7
   The Sickness of Tristram.. 8
   The Death of Launcelot... 9
LATER VERSE AND PROGRAM NOTES 12
   The Old Man in the Night... 13
Joan and the Bells (Program Notes)....................................... 17
   Part One: Judgment... 19
   Part Two: Joan in Her Chamber.................................... 21
   Part Three: The Square at Rouen 23
Young America (Program Notes)... 27
   Hark the Homeland.. 28
   Heather Mary.. 28
   My Uncle's House.. 30
   Daughter of Asheville... 30
   When Daniel Boone Goes By at Night........................... 31
Three Welsh Songs (Program Notes)..................................... 32
   Welcome, Robin... 33
   Kind Old Man 34
   All Through the Night... 37
Poor Peter Cycle (Program Notes).. 39
   Where Is My Lady?.. 40
   Tune the Fiddle.. 40
   The Ballad of Poor Peter 41

Various Choral Pieces (Album Notes) 43
    Beauty Come Dancing 45
    The Old Man in the Morning 46
    Shenandoah 47
Four Christmas Carols (Program Notes) 49
    Call the Children 49
    The Snow Child 50
    Run to the Window 50
    Candles on the Tree 51
Gretchen to Faust (Program Notes) 53
    Gretchen to Faust 53
Mephistopheles to Faust (Program Notes) 55
    Mephistopheles to Faust 55
The Old Man in the Snow (Program Notes) 57
    The Old Man in the Snow 57

AUTHOR'S NOTES ON THE FOUR LIBRETTI 59

Plump Jack (Program Notes) 63
Plump Jack (Synopsis) 69
    Plump Jack (Libretto) 73
Usher House (Program Notes) 141
Usher House (Synopsis) 142
    Usher House (Libretto) 145
The Canterville Ghost (Program Notes) 169
The Canterville Ghost (Synopsis) 171
    The Canterville Ghost (Libretto) 176
Goodbye, Mr. Chips (Program Notes) 201
Goodbye, Mr. Chips (Synopsis) 203
    Goodbye, Mr. Chips (Libretto) 206

AFTERWORD BY THE AUTHOR 241

Praise for Gordon Getty's *UPON A DAY*

"The richness of Mr. Getty's language—its classical models audible even in his contemporary subjects, his images no less evocative for being expressed in the most lucid prose and verse forms—could only be the work of a composer as passionate about the music in his words themselves, as well as that music he composes to illuminate and complete them. An indispensable introduction to the artist's work."

~John Corigliano, Composer

"The extraordinary Gordon Getty is a deeply gifted and prolific composer with a poet's heart and soul: there is great poetry in his music, and profound music in his verse. This vibrant collection makes clear that his enthusiasm and passion for form, structure, invention, and beautiful language inhabits every part of his creative psyche. Getty's poetic voice, authentically and memorably his own, glows with the resonance of greats like Keats, Dickinson, and Whitman."

~Jake Heggie, Composer

"Anyone who knows Gordon Getty is in awe of his intelligence, humor, and continued journey into every corner of the world that he has explored. I am in awe of his heart as well, and of his devotion to humanity. Reading his poetry and librettos takes one to another state, one of awe to be sure, but also one of deep and profound respect: respect for learning, for discovery, for appreciation of all that is around us. And he reminds us that it is all around us! He teaches us to 'teach ourselves' and then does even more to 'mend the world.'"

~Frederica von Stade, Mezzo-Soprano

"We composers might take a cue from Gordon Getty and, if we have the capacity, write our own libretti. The texts he has penned fit his music impulses hand-in-glove, as anyone who has encountered his operas and song cycles can attest. In his settings he is not afraid to speak directly, does not shy away from the sentimental, nor is he averse to entertaining both the listener and the reader."

~John Adams, Composer

"What I admire about Gordon, both as a human being and as a writer, is his passion. He is a tireless enthusiast, and that fuels everything he does whether as a writer or a composer. He is quite irresistible."

~Stephen Rubin, Publisher, Author, Music Critic

We sadly lost our beloved colleague and friend, Steve Rubin. He was a force of nature, a brilliant publisher, and encyclopedic in his knowledge of music. His boundless passion inspired all of us, and his legacy of endless laughter and profound humanity will endure through time.

"There are qualities in the writing of Gordon Getty that the world needs more of these days: warmth, tenderness, nobility, humanity. That is why reading his work is ultimately such a gratifying experience."

~Henry Fogel, Arts Executive and Consultant

"What a balm for the world Gordon Getty's poetry and prose bestows on us. While looking at the richness of the human experience—rife with its shifting shades of dark and light—there is always comfort present, offering itself generously to those in need. The gentle understanding and worldly wisdom that pour out of his writing changes you for the better."

~Joyce DiDonato, Mezzo-Soprano

INTRODUCTION BY THE AUTHOR

I can't remember when I wasn't composing verse and music. My nephew Mark Getty found some of the poems included here, including "The Death of Launcelot" and "The Old Man in the Night," and published them privately, in 150 copies, as a gift for my fiftieth birthday. Some of these, and most of the later poems, have been published in my musical settings on the Pentatone label.

Let me be judged by any of them. But if I could publish only a few, those few would include "The Death of Launcelot," "Heather Mary," the "Poor Peter" cycle, "Beauty Come Dancing," the three "Old Man" poems, and the two adaptations from *Faust*. It happens that I have set all of this special group to music except "The Death of Launcelot." Since I have also set some outside that group, why not this one within it, or anyhow not yet?

Reason might infer that verse left unset must be inferior as less worth setting, or superior as less in need of setting. The truth, I think, is that music and verse stand outside the jurisdiction of reason. Reason processes only a part of them. They come from somewhere in Freud's id, or Plato's cave, to help us see what reason alone cannot. It was Thomas Carlisle, I think, who wrote that the Germanic tribes weighed matters of state once at lunch when all were sober, then once again at dinner when all were drunk, and took action only if both verdicts agreed. Music and verse, at their best, are the wine or mead that reminds sweet reason of things outside its reach.

A boy isn't likely to take an interest in opera until his voice changes, at age 13, say, so that he can identify more easily with the characters. It was at about that age that I began staying awake when my mother took me and my older brother Paul and younger sister Donna to the opera. I began collecting opera records out of my allowance, particularly of Björling, Caruso, and McCormack. I suppose it had occurred to me all along that I might end up writing an opera, and maybe its libretto too.

So it happened, although other things came first. I'll say more about my operas and libretti when we come to them in the second part of this book. One thing to say now is that the secrets of verse and prose are about the same but with different emphasis. For verse, too, the sound is part of the meaning. This is the part that we feel, rather than see, and which guides judgment in ways not wholly understood.

The music of Gordon Getty can be heard on Spotify, Apple Music or other streaming or downloading websites.

VERSE FROM COLLEGE AND BACHELOR DAYS

These verses date from the late 1940s through the early 1960s. I experimented more then, trying different styles and personae. Now I try to adapt the persona a little more to me, and me a little less to the persona. That said, I was the same poet then as now. I've changed a few words to fit my new approach, but not many.

"My Uncle's House," which appears first in this group, hints of James Whitcomb Riley in subject, if less in style. George Lewis, in the second poem, was a jazz clarinetist known to me only through recordings. Jazz isn't my thing, but this guy impressed me. The tentative "somewhat" in the last line suggests a touch of Prufrock in the speaker. The sendup of Eliot in the fourth poem was an in-joke among classmates; Eliot was no more a plagiarist than poets should be.

The second of the two elegies paraphrases Somerset Maugham. "Saint Christopher" owes a bow to Cowper's majestic line "He plants His footsteps in the sea." "The Sickness of Tristram" followed my first experience of *Tristan und Isolde* at the War Memorial Opera House in San Francisco. Kirsten Flagstad, by gosh, sang Isolde! The poem suggests the prelude to Act III, and the lines of Tristan and Kurwenal immediately following. Its dactyls and alliteration pay respect to the poetic manner of the time.

"The Death of Launcelot," although placed in the same time, chooses the gentler ballad form of iambs in four feet and three. Almesbury, the River Malvern, and the Marian sisterhood are all made up as far as I can tell. If any exist, my apologies for misdescribing them, as I must have done.

My Uncle's House

My uncle's house had eaves of white
And studs all plush with creepers;
We rucked the ground from break of light
And sang the Dutch songs late at night,
For we were noisy girls and boys,
And those who didn't like the noise
Learned to be heavy sleepers.

When strangers thought it wearying
That we should sing so much,
Then we would say we had hoped, come spring,
To teach the gophers how to sing
And teach the crickets Dutch.

My uncle died, my sisters wed,
I and my cousins moved to town,
And the old house was taken down.
It was a place, my uncle said,
For keeping cheer with live and dead,
For song by night and work by morn,
A place for being born.

I wish my sons no finer birth;
I wish them this, to find
How patience and the generous earth
Make life, how work makes wealth and worth,
And song the gracèd mind.

A Group of Children Playing the Game "Oranges and Lemons" in a Domestic Interior
Harry Brooker

George Lewis

George Lewis, though I never knew
What faculty of mind and hand
Made music, nor which part was planned
And which part self-conceiving grew,
Yet this at least I understand:
The laughter of your tumbling word
Stopped, and will not again be heard,
And somewhat darker is the land.

George Lewis: photo from the Redfern Collection / JP Jazz Archive / Getty Images

Sonnet

How shall I learn to see with poets' eyes?
What shall I value, I who never saw
A simple life teach grace, or reason law,
Or faith content men, sorrow make them wise?
I have seen beauty, although beauty dies,
I have seen peace, while war was drawing breath;
I have not seen the love more strong than death
But I have seen the love that laughs and cries,

I have seen youth his metal, age his rust,
And poets, I have seen your books, and known
Nothing on earth more worthy to be shown;
For if I, looking with you, see but half,
He who sees most sees best, and when I laugh
It is the laughter of most childlike trust.

On T.S. Eliot

Alderman, *n.* An ingenious criminal who covers his
    secret thieving with a pretence of open maraud-
    ing. "The Devil's Dictionary," Ambrose Bierce.

Now here's a song for Possum Bellyache.
Where is old Possum? Bilge and Boulders!
He's got Kit Marlowe by the shoulders,
Nor spares to move ye stones and bones
And Holy Writ he superzones.
He joggles Dante by the heels
And wears right proudly what he steals.
But if he filch with such éclat,
Now really, where's the harm in that?
For lift he left or rob he right,
He always keeps his hands in sight.
His hands, that is–but never close
Your eyes on his prehensile toes.

Two Elegies

1. The breath is out, the miracle unmade.

2. Knowing this is being wise,
   Man is born, he lives, he dies,
   Man lives and dies and man is born,
   We shall not mourn.

St. Christopher

The birds and I
Are born to die
But we have the sky
And a place to sleep.
God keeps the shore,
God holds the sea,
In time before,
In time to be,
His hand is set upon the deep
And in His purpose He will keep.

Photo by Frank McKenna

The Sickness of Tristram

Hard by the castle high on the hillcrest over the water,
Tristram of Lyonesse gray with his death-wound lay.

The willow leaf rode wide on the wind, and a single
seabird called.

Ever Lord Tristram spoke in that witchery Northern tongue,
    and ever repeated an alien name in a voice like a
        sifting of winds.

Great sorrow to think of that Tristram's voice once singing
    through shocks, rallying ranks, shaking the great of
        the field.

Time upon time he would summon me: "True friend, for else
    I am friendless,

Take thou the watch, seek out the ship, call to me quickly,
    tell me how distant –

I say I have seen the bright sail bend, the white prow
    breaking the billows,

Coming with her of the tresses of light, she mystical-trancing,
    dew-handed subduer of suffering,

Coming with old hearts free of this region of time death-meshed,
    of perpetual dying,

Of things death enters so warily none know when he
    is come,

Of things death enters each day like a fog, so we know not
    where he is lighted,

While the willow leaf rides wide on the wind, and a
    single seabird calls."

The Death of Launcelot

From Almesbury to southward
   And west, the Malvern flows
Through valleys every-colored
   Or smoothèd thick with snows,

And there the Marian sisters
   Have kept a convent fair
To which in all of England
   None other can compare

For walks and pools and gardens,
   For breezes from the sea,
For morning song and evening song,
   For gracious company.

When first they brought the Queen there
   All beautiful and wild
She never spoke to any
   And neither wept nor smiled,

But as each season came anew
And her dark hour more distant drew
She sang their songs at times, and grew
   To learn their manners mild,

Until her early kingdom
   Began to seem a word
Of an uncertain meaning,
   Once in a fever heard.

It was a Lenten Sunday,
   The fields were quick with spring,
While voices sang from grass and tree,
   From water and from wing;
The sisters sang about Our Lord,
   And likewise she did sing.

Somewhat beyond the noontide
   An aged penitent,
Borne thither, asked to see her,
   So straightaway she went.

He was so white and withered
   That he might seem to be
A spirit without body,
   A soul already free,

Yet when she saw, she knew him
   And of a sudden thought
That something might unfasten
   The peace that had been brought,

The quiet ways, the gardens;
   So that she paused in fear
A step from where he lay. He said,
   Not moving, "You are here."

Once was his voice a music
   Of eagles and the sea;
Now his words fell as leaves fall
   In autumn from a tree.

She took his hand. The birds sang
   In branches overhead.
She said, "We are so changed now."
   "Yes, we are changed," he said,

"The world is made to vanish,
   A kingdom is a breath,
But lady, I have loved you
   Beyond the power of death.

It was great pain to love you,
   From the first hour I knew,
Great pain and greater evil
   By all that I held true,

By vows, by God's commandment,
   By fealty forsworn,
By treason to the saintliest man
   Since Christ, that had been born;

Great pain, and greater evil,
   For even then I saw
The ruin that would follow,
   The wrecking of the law,

Yet I could not forsake you
   Nor even wish to die,
But only wish to hold you
   Beneath another sky,

Southward, or in the lake-land
   From which my fathers came;
Somewhere to lie beside you,
   To hear you speak my name."

He paused, and lay all silent
   Within that westward light;
Now only moved the shadow-hand
That pulls upon both sea and land
   The coverlet of night.

She waited; still the birds sang
   Unseen in branches round,
Then thought she of a colder place
   And of a louder sound,
A name by many thousands cried
Where one man evenly did ride
   Upon a battleground.

How greatly she had loved him!
   Once when he rode to war
She well might weep for pride and fear,
   But this was long before,
A time of what was won and lost
   And now would come no more,

So that as he had spoken,
   The love of which he told
Seemed to belong to others.
   She thought, "Have I grown old?"

He pressed her hand. The shadows
   Drew quietly about
When in a sudden moment
   She thought his life went out,

Yet it ran backward quickly;
   He drew her close beside;
And said, "I loved none other."
   "Nor I none," she replied,
"In all the world." She kissed him
   Most gently as he died.

She closed his eyes and blessed him,
   She called the sisters round,
And said, "Sir Launcelot du Lac
   Shall lie in holy ground."

They bore him to the chapel
   And knelt with her to pray
In silence, in the twilight
   That brings out night from day,

Then was the vesper-hour begun,
And many voices drew to one.

The Death of Sir Lancelot • Historica Graphica Collection / Heritage Images:
From Stories of the Knights of the Round Table by Henry Gilbert, first edition, 1911

LATER VERSE AND PROGRAM NOTES

For whatever reason, I completed no music or verse for eighteen years after finishing my two courses at the San Francisco Conservatory of Music in 1962. That changed when I bought a copy of Emily Dickinson's poems in 1980 while on summer vacation in Paris with my wife and boys, and began to set some in my head. Verse and music came easily enough after that.

My first completed texts in this second period include "The Old Man in the Night" and *Usher House*, which was meant to work as a short play as well as a libretto. Next came the verse to "Joan and the Bells" in loose iambic pentameter with dactyls at the end. I had thought about writing an opera on Joan, and another on Anne Frank, since college days. Nothing came of the Anne Frank project except for the first four lines of "Saint Christopher" (on page 7), which were originally meant for her. The outcome here as to Joan amounts to three operatic scenes. As set, it is probably best described as a cantata with soloists and chorus.

The verse for "My Uncle's House" (shown on p.4), the third part of my *Young America* cycle, was written in college days. "The Ballad of Poor Peter," in my *Poor Peter* cycle, develops from a version also written in college. The version shown here adds enough to count it as new.

The Old Man in the Night
1982

He was an old man, slow but straight; his head
Looked set on something far. Perhaps he thought
I had gone with the rest, but I had stayed
A rise above him, with young pines between,
To watch the sun fall. Now at last it caught
Something at sea, then windows on a street
Far off, and made them flash across the park
Blood molten; now the light leapt molten green
To sea again, then spilling in retreat,
Now foot by foot stretched thinner, tangled, frayed,
Guttered, the huge sun drowning, burning dark.

I meant to go, but then the old man said
"I have come back. It is the day, the place,
And now the hour. There, it was there she turned
And looked at me. We walked again. Her hair
Blew round her like a fire; the late light burned
In her hair's colors, fire-like, just as these.
My friends and I were silent. No man there
Had seen such beauty; I have seen none since,
Beauty to stop men's hearts and turn men white,
Beauty to mute the watcher and to bind,
Beauty to make him feel both clod and prince,
Beauty to crown and beggar at its ease.
For how could such as we return such grace?
Then each man knew allegiance in his mind,
And each man thought, "Well, Lady, I have sworn
To love and serve you to the Judgment Morn.'
But she had looked at me."
 I had no right,
I knew, to hear such things. What spectral tryst
Had I profaned? For she of whom he spoke
Was now forever in some way his own,
And not for strangers. Yet I could not go
Unheard; the walks were gravel. It grew late.
The sun fell, now a star came, now a mist,

Then other stars. Surely he need not know.
Much better he should think himself alone;
Much better that it were not I who broke
That silence. Let that sundown hour long past
Be his unshared for keeping. I could wait.
Then he said,
                   "It was here I sought at last
The kindly night, with thoughts not to be told,
The kindly night, lest men should see and muse,
'It is the grief that Adam knew of old,
Who learned and lost.' For grief is from the first,
And sorrow the old coinage men must use
To pay tuition as they learn the law
Of time exacting, time that takes his due,
Time that will have the best and leave the worst,
Of time that garners beauty as he must,
Of time most certain. Then at length I saw
That sorrow is a precious thing whereby
Beauty can stay awhile and may hold true,
That beauty gone may live in sorrow's trust,
In sorrow and the night until we die.
And so I walked, and thought the night a friend
Worthy to keep all secrets to the end."

This hint alarmed me. Had he found me out?
I felt a fool, though I had meant the best.
I could feign waking as from sleep, then leave.
A silly game, yet better to deceive
Than make things worse. Then as I sat in doubt
He spoke again, and put my doubt to rest.
He could not know, for what he said made clear
That none alive save he was meant to hear:

"O beautiful my love, it is the hour
To beauty sacred, beauty consecrate,
It is the night, that gathers in her reach
Things past, things coming. Years fall, centuries
Fall and are counted, but the night is one;
We and Orion and the Pleiades,

The Herdsman and his flock, the Huntress Moon
Touch and are one. Now time yields up his power;
Now hasten, beauty, his hand drops, he frees
The prisoner decades, all is rebegun;
We and the Huntress and her prey above
All rebegun, renewed. O beauty lost,
O beauty lithe and delicate, come soon,
Make speed, O dextrous, beauty stepping light,
Sure-footed beauty, come, O come in state,
Come conquer, O majestic, reign and teach,
O beauty, come in the archaic night,
Beauty beyond all keeping, worth all cost,
O beautiful and merciless my love."

JOAN AND THE BELLS

Johanna of Orleans • Raymond Balze

Joan and the Bells (Program Notes)

1429 was the 92nd year of the Hundred Years' War. Three generations of French had been bloodied in the disasters of Crecy, Poitiers and Agincourt. In the spring of that year an illiterate peasant girl told first the Governor of her region, and then the Dauphin, that she had been chosen by God to drive the English back to their shores. She was given a few soldiers and sent to join the defense of Orleans. She led the French army to victory. Later in that year she broke the English strongholds along the Loire, and led the Dauphin through Burgundian territory to his coronation at Rheims.

Soon she had proved too warlike and independent for the new king's comfort. In 1430 she attacked Burgundian Paris, without result, after he had declared a truce. When she was captured in battle a few months later he did not ransom her, although he could have done so easily under the customs of the time. She was sold to the Duke of Burgundy, and tried by the Church for heresy and witchcraft at Rouen in 1431. Pierre Cauchon, the Bishop of Beauvais, led the prosecution. She renounced her visions under a promise that her life would be spared, and recanted on learning that the terms included life imprisonment on bread and water. She was now trapped as a relapsed heretic, and was burned at the stake. She was about nineteen years old.

Myth can add little to such a history. Like other writers, even so, I have cast Joan's story in a myth to suit my telling. *Joan and the Bells* keeps to some facts and makes up others. Thus Domremy is given a Lourdes-like setting for picturesqueness alone. It is true meanwhile that church bells brought Joan's visions and voices, but not that any were silenced at her trial. It is true that her banner read "Jesu Maria," and that lip-readers made out her last words to be "Jesu, Jesu."

There is also no reason to suppose that Cauchon was compassionate in the end. He is made so here to mitigate Church-bashing, to give the benefit of the doubt to little-known historical figures, and to keep the focus on Joan. Her story needs no villains. It is the hero, not the saint, who is measured by the size of the dragon slain. The saint is measured by the promise kept, by the beauty of the vision, and by the straightness of the path.

Schiller and Mark Twain, and Verdi and Tchaikovsky, made Joan wise beyond her years. Indeed she was. The record of her trial, which was meticulous by the standards of the time, shows a defendant of acumen and poise. People grew up fast in her age of war and freebooters and the Black Death. It was the genius of Shaw that inverted this safe literary tradition and brought out the spunky teenager in Joan. Jean Anouilh went farther, in *The Lark*, and gave her the simplicity of preadolescence. *Joan and the Bells* owes much to these masters, particularly Anouilh, and takes the same poetic license. It is a tale of a child's faith in an age without childhood, of a valor undeflected, and of the redemption these qualities commend.

Joan and the Bells
1995

Part One: Judgment

CAUCHON AND MONKS
Joan the Maid, you are condemned.
You have done prodigies by witchcraft,
Beyond all temporal power, in men's clothes,
You have led armies and defeated armies,
And counseled heresies. You have heard our judgment.
Let it be entered.

JOAN
I wore men's clothes and armor
And fought their fight.
God put a sword into my hand.

MONKS
She is blaspheming. Silence her.

CAUCHON
You are mistaken. Satan armed you, child.
The sword was his. Repent, be healed, be saved.
Cast him away, and you will bless our judgment.
Receive God's grace, and you will bless the flames;
Let God's grace shine in them and sing in them,
Let them drive out the husk, the dross, the slag,
Let them drive out that antichrist, the mortal world,
Let them refine, cleanse, cauterize,
Let them anneal, let them distill,
Let them make pure. Renounce your visions,
Know them aright. They are not your three saints.
You have confessed that these things are not saints
But Satan and his minions.

JOAN
I thank the court. Your Reverences
Are old and wise, the Church is God's true agent,
And I am perjured.
I was afraid, and was not true to them,
Saint Catherine, Saint Margaret, Saint Michael,
I did them evil,
Here in this room I called them frauds and specters,
But I have asked their pardon,
And must not wrong them more.
Your Reverences have sentenced me most justly.
I am still wicked and afraid.
But, Reverences, I must not wrong them more,
And I will ask their pardon in the fire.

MONKS
Defiance! Blasphemy! Brothers, you are too patient.

CAUCHON
She is obdurate. We can do nothing.
Remove her. Pray for her. The trial is closed.
There was no fault in it. God help us now,
But, Brothers, who can say we were not fair?
We were most circumspect. The pope absolves us.
The laity consent.

MONKS
Thus far.
But there must be no bells.

CAUCHON
There will be none.
The Duke of Bedford stilled them.

MONKS
They are her voices.

CAUCHON
He took their tongues.

MONKS
Her visions come with them.

CAUCHON
The bells are mute. God help us, Brothers,
But who can say we were not fair?

MONKS
Who can say we were not fair?

Part Two: Joan in Her Chamber

JOAN
Saint Margaret, I ask your pardon first,
Because it was you I saw the first of all,
Running to church. Do you remember?
It was fall and cool and morning and beautiful;
I was running up where the path was highest,
Up where the bells came loudest, on the hillside,
In the forest by the spring,
Where I could see our roof and all the roofs,
But this time I was running not to be late,
And did not look.
Do you remember? All at once I saw you,
As plain as anyone, but beautiful and shining,
And I knew you were a saint.
Then I saw you, Saint Michael,
And you, Saint Catherine,
And now I ask your pardon too. I am ashamed,
For I have broken faith with you,
And made you angry,
And that is why you will not come to me.

But then you came, all three,
And, Blessed Margaret, you said,
"Joan, do you know us?" And I said,
"I do, Saint Margaret,
But I think you must have lost your way.

Not even the abbé comes to Domremy."
Saint Michael, then you said, "Joan,
Are you afraid of us?" And I said, "No, Saint Michael,"
And then, Saint Catherine, you said,
"It is good that you are not,
For you must ride a horse, and be a soldier,
And hold a sword." And I said, "Oh, Saint Catherine,
A soldier?" And you answered,
"If you are not afraid, and keep your word,
And do your very best,
Then you will be a soldier, and ride a horse,
And hold a sword, and crown a king,
And do brave things that will be told forever."
And I said, "Well, then, I will try,
But how can I do all of that?"
And then, Saint Michael, you said,
"You will know how, all by yourself,
And when you need us we will come to you."

Oh, blessed saints, it was the truth.
At Chinon Castle you led me to the Dauphin
And made him trust me. At Orleans
Where we had fought all day without advantage,
And had fallen back to garrison as weak as death,
You came and said that we must try once more.
Somehow I made them do it, and we won.
So it was on the Loire,
At Meung, Jargeau, Patay, so many times,
Whenever we were nearly broken,
With fresh reserves against us, banners high,
Mocking at us, our ordnance driven back,
Dust-blind, our force encircled, then you came
In our great need, just as you said,
To give me courage, and the field was ours.
Even when I was taken at Compiègne,
And even here, you came to me each day,
But now I have been untruthful,
And that is why you will not speak to me.
Dear saints, I will do better,

There is only a little time, but I will try,
And then perhaps you will not be so angry,
And you will come to me.

Part Three: The Square at Rouen

MOST TOWNSFOLK
They are building the fire too high.
The executioner will not be able to come near,
Once it is lit,
To do the act of mercy.
It is cruel.

CAUCHON (aside)
Yes, it is cruel.

MONKS AND OTHER TOWNSFOLK
It is justice. She is a witch.
She is a heretic relapsed.

VARIOUS GROUPS OF TOWNSFOLK
She is young and beautiful.

I do not think she is a witch.

She is not afraid. She is very calm.

CAUCHON (aside)
Her head is high.

VARIOUS GROUPS OF TOWNSFOLK
She is a witch. The court condemned her.

Now they will light the fire. It is lit.
The flames are terrible.

Listen! There are bells. I hear them.

Yes! There are bells.

MONKS, etc.
There are no bells. Lord Bedford took their tongues.
Sometimes the bells can bring her visions to her.
That is why he made them mute.

MOST TOWNSFOLK
They are not the bells of Rouen.

CAUCHON (aside)
No, they are other bells. I heard them once,
When I was very young.

VARIOUS GROUPS OF TOWNSFOLK
They are other bells.

There are no bells. Lord Bedford stilled them.

She is looking at something up high.

What is it?

She is watching the tower.

No, she is looking above it.

Her lips are moving.
She is praying. I cannot make out the words.
What does she say?

CAUCHON (aside)
She is saying, "Jesu, Jesu, Jesu."

CHORUS (ANGELS)
Come, child, come, soldier,
The task is finished, finished and settled away,
It is all mended and folded away,
The battle is done with, over and gone,

And washed away with the morning.
You have won and rested. Listen! The bells!
See, you have won, child! Now rise up
In the cool of the morning, run to us,
Run up in the cool hills, run barefoot, run, child, feel the wind,
Feel the cool wind, run higher, higher,
Up to the mountaintops, higher!
Jump higher than the world! The bells are louder!
Here, child! Faster! See, you are almost home!
Up here, child! Run up to the sky and past it,
Past clouds and moons and comets,
Up, child! It is so blue and bright!
You can hardly see! Brighter and brighter!

Come running, riding; now you are riding, child!
Ride forward, faster, faster, higher, higher,
Up to the front, child!
See the battalions align, there are Dunois, LaHire,
In the cool of the morning, Xantrailles and his lancers,
The ground is resilient, quick for the charge,
See the horses, the riders, the ranks,
How they quiver and quicken, their eyes, they are ready,
All of them furious, dangerous, ready,
Spur, child! Up to the gallop, apace, hear the war-shout,
The banner, aloft! Let it fly, let it carry them,
Jesu Maria, they see it, they follow,
Attack, child! Into the enemy, at them!
Into the cavalry, up to the cannon, the colors!
The bells are everywhere!
See, the gates open, child, the pennants fall, the captains kneel!
Ride up, child, up to the battlements, up to the stars,
Ride up in the cool of the morning.

YOUNG AMERICA

Engraving from the collection of bauhaus1000 / iStock.com

Young America (Program Notes)

Stephen Vincent Benét has given more to these poems than the closing quatrain. "Hark the Homeland" is modeled on the opening pages of *John Brown's Body*, and is the first part of my homage here to this neglected master. I wrote the text of "Heather Mary" on safari in 1997, and of "Daughter of Asheville" and "Hark the Homeland" a few months later. "My Uncle's House" goes back to my college days. I began writing the music for all but "Daughter of Asheville" a few days before the September 11 atrocities, and finished within three weeks while also putting in full days at the office. Busy times.

Poetry is meant to be cryptic. If you understand everything, or even if I do, I have failed. "Heather Mary" is set in the British Isles some two or three centuries ago, by the sound of it, when emigration was a daily topic and the new world less defined. Heather Mary and Little Jamie are perhaps eight or nine years old. What they say reminds us that children can know the meaning of a promise, better than we, and know the things that end with time, and the things that do not.

Where that song is a poem set to music, "Daughter of Asheville" is a lyric set to a tune I thought up years before. Both the words and the music of the latter are meant to sound as if they might have been written during the Civil War. What can we guess of Janet Alicia and her dancing partner? I think we are being told that he died in the Battle of the Wilderness, with her name on his lips. I would conjecture that she died generations later, in a world of motorcars and relativity, surrounded by their children and grandchildren and great-grandchildren, with his ring on her finger. Now they dance, with the merry and brave, seeing only each other, into a dawn past reach.

Benét's great miniature "When Daniel Boone Goes By at Night" reverses the time-line and takes us back to the forest primeval in which "Hark the Homeland" began. What an ear! The unexpected spondee in "all lost wild America," and the warmth and wit of the whole, make the piece a prize in any company. All a composer need do with such a text is to get out of its way.

Young America
Poems by Gordon Getty and Stephen Vincent Benét
2001

Hark the Homeland
(by Gordon Getty)

Hark the homeland, hear it calling,
Listen back and catch the echo,
Hear the piping, hear the war-song,
Paiute, Chippewa, Tuskeeegee,
Then the axe, the adze, the hammer,
Next the barnyard, shipyard, steelyard,
Now the Iron Horse, the freeway,
Hark the homeland.

Hear the wholeness, good and evil,
Something dangerous, uncharted,
Headlong, headstrong in the darkness,
Hear the ocean in the darkness,
Hear the psalms, the chains, the shanties,
Hear the German, Erse, Italian,
Cantonese, Sicilian, Farsi,
Hear the journey in the darkness,
Hark the homeland.

Heather Mary
(by Gordon Getty)

"If I go across the sea,
Jamie, will you follow me?"

"Heather Mary, when I grow,
Point your foot and I will go."

"Jamie, if I cross the sea,
Will you find and marry me?"

"Path and penfold, hill and hollow,
Where your foot goes I will follow,
Left and right,
Across the world from side to side,
And where the sun goes in the night,
And you will be my bride."

"Jamie, you cannot live on air,
How will you earn, and pay the fare,
And find me there?"

"Well, I will work, and do my best,
And build a boat and sail it west
And I will know,
For people who have seen you go
Will sing of you, and by the song
Will mark where you have walked along."

"What if you find, when you are done,
And come to me beyond the sun,
That I have wed another one?"

"Then Heather Mary, I will know
That once I have seen beauty go."

"Well, Jamie, I will wait for you
And marry none beside,
And you will know the way,
And come to me, and have me true,
But if I die before,
For other hands to bury,
Then you must find the stone
And write that you have loved none more
But me alone."

"Then, Heather Mary, I will go
Across the ocean when I grow
To marry you, but if you die,
Then I will find you where you lie
And write upon the stone to say:
'This was the lady of the grace,
My only bride,
Her name was Heather Mary,
And we who saw her face
Will know the beauty of this place.'"

My Uncle's House
(Poem found on p.4)

Daughter of Asheville
(by Gordon Getty)

Dance with me, daughter of Asheville,
Dance in the candlelight, dance in my dreams,
Dance in the white of the moon.
Dreams and the music will die in the morning,
The candle will yield to the shadow too soon,
Dance with me, daughter of Asheville,
Dance in the white of the moon.

O my beloved, remember,
Honor the word that we spoke to the stars,
Keep to the promise we gave.
Come to me, beauty, come dance with me, beauty,
Come dance in the wilderness where I must go,
Dance with me, Janet Alicia,
Dance in the wind and the snow.

Now and forever come with me, my darling,
Come hold me, my darling,
Come dance with the dancers, the merry and brave,

Oh my beloved, remember,
Keep to the promise we gave.

Dance with me, daughter of Asheville,
Dance in the candlelight, dance in my dreams,
Dance in the white of the moon.
Dreams and the music will die in the morning,
The candle will yield to the shadow too soon,
Dance with me, daughter of Asheville,
Dance in the white of the moon.

When Daniel Boone Goes By at Night
(by Stephen Vincent Benét)

When Daniel Boone goes by, at night,
The phantom deer arise,
And all lost, wild America
Is burning in their eyes.

DANIEL BOONE by Stephen Vincent Benét
from A BOOK OF AMERICANS by Rosemary and Stephen Vincent Benét.
Henry Holt and Company, Inc.
Copyright 1933 by Rosemary and Stephen Vincent Benét
Copyright © renewed 1961 by Rosemary Carr Benét.

Three Welsh Songs (**Program Notes**)

I am the world's worst singer, unless your hat is in the ring. I always wanted to sing "All Through the Night," and bought an anthology including it. The English translation given there may have been faithful to the Welsh, for all I know, but was pretty clumsy after the first four lines. The arrangement was plain, with a nice use of parallel thirds and sixths in lines four and five. I kept the four good lines and the parallel thirds and sixths, and the glorious tune itself, and otherwise started from scratch.

"Welcome, Robin" and "Kind Old Man" were in the same anthology, again with simple accompaniments. "Welcome, Robin" already had a charming text and tune, and needed only more harmony and counterpoint. "Kind Old Man" is a wonderful nonsense song, alternating between doleful and lively refrains. I added still more nonsense to the words, and hammed up the slow parts with barbershop melisma and melodrama. Keep the text in front of you, since I have asked the singers to take the fast parts *presto possibile*.

"All Through the Night," of course, is the closer. I intended the text as a lyric, with a common touch, rather than a stand-alone poem. I chose hymn-like harmonies, more or less inevitably, but added a counter-melody in broken chords to bring out the bardic potential.

Three Welsh Songs
New English lyrics by Gordon Getty
2004

Welcome, Robin

Welcome, Robin, with thy greeting,
On the threshold meekly waiting,
To the children's home now enter
From the cold and snow of winter.
From the cold and snow of winter.

Art thou cold? Or art thou hungry?
Pretty Robin, don't be angry.
All the children round thee rally.
While the snow is in the valley.
While the snow is in the valley.

Robin, come and tell thy story,
Leave outside thy care and worry,
Tell the children, Robin dearest,
Of the babies in the forest.
Of the babies in the forest.

Kind Old Man

Where have you been wand'ring, kind old man,
The kindest man alive?
"I went out a-fishin', boys,
Fal-dee-ree-dee-ree-do,
Made 'em pay admission, boys,
Fal-dee-ree-dee-ree-do,
Boiled 'em in me hat, boys,
Fal-dee-ree-dee-riddle-o,
Sold 'em to the cat, boys,
Fal-dee-ree-dee-riddle-o,
What d'ya think of that, boys,
Fal-dee-ree-dee, heigh ho!"

Why are you shivering, kind old man,
The kindest man alive?
"I fell into a ditch, boys,
Fal-dee-ree-dee-ree-do,
Can't remember which, boys,
Fal-dee-ree-dee-ree-do,
Caught a lovely cold, boys,
Fal-dee-ree-dee-riddle-o,
Comes from getting old, boys,
Fal-dee-ree-dee-riddle-o,
Worth its weight in gold, boys,
Fal-dee-ree-dee, kachoo!

What if you get a fever, kind old man,
The kindest man alive?
"I'll have to take the cure, boys,
Fal-dee-ree-dee-ree-do,
Keeps the system pure, boys,
Fal-dee-ree-dee-ree-do,
Circulate the jug, boys,
Fal-dee-ree-dee-riddle-o,
Take another tug, boys,
Fal-dee-ree-dee-riddle-o,
Throw away the plug, boys,
Fal-dee-ree-dee, here's how!"

What if you should die then, kind old man,
The kindest man alive?
"Then bury me in state, boys,
Fal-dee-ree-dee-ree-do,
Underneath the grate, boys,
Fal-dee-ree-dee-ree-do,
To hear the porridge bubble, boys,
Fal-dee-ree-dee-riddle-o,
Thank you for your trouble, boys,
Fal-dee-ree-dee-riddle-o,
Pour another double, boys,
Fal-dee-ree-dee, God bless!"

Good Night • © Edgar Jerins/artlicensing.com

All Through the Night

Sleep, my love, and peace attend thee,
All through the night.
Guardian angels God will lend thee
All through the night.
Hushed, the world lies lost in sleeping,
Hushed the harvest, hushed its reaping,
Hushed the stars their vigil keeping,
All through the night.

Once I told my love in sorrow
All through the night,
Long the waiting, cold the morrow
All through the night,
Sleep, my love, and dreams will bring thee
Clothes of starry wreathes to ring thee,
Angel choirs their songs to sing thee,
All through the night.

Come the kings and come the lowly,
All through the night,
Keep the watch and keep it holy,
All through the night.
Voices from the dreamland woken,
She will hear your words unspoken,
Hold her in your pledge unbroken,
All through the night.

The Lute Player • Frans Hals

Poor Peter Cycle (Program Notes)

Poor Peter is set in the Middle Ages of myth, of Sherwood Forest or Camelot or Christmas carols. "Where is My Lady," which opens the cycle, also appears in my opera *Usher House*. There it is sung by the narrator, who I make to be Poe himself, and then reprised wordlessly by Madeline as she walks up from her crypt at the end. The "Beauty and grace …" refrain, although not so much the whole poem, is meant to sound as if Poe might have written it.

"Tune the Fiddle" offers a foot-stomping contrast in tempo and dynamic, and gives a hint of the sass and cheek expected of actual minstrels in festive songs. Minstrels seem to have been a rowdy lot, incidentally, judging from *Grove's*.

The main idea of "The Ballad of Poor Peter" comes from Yeats' "The Song of Wandering Aengus," where a girl materializes magically, runs off, and is followed by Aengus forever:

> "Though I am old with wandering,
> Through hollow lands and hilly lands,
> I will find out where she has gone,
> And kiss her lips and take her hands;
> And walk among long-dappled grass,
> And pluck, till time and times are done,
> The silver apples of the moon,
> The golden apples of the sun."

The debt of my own lines to this, particularly in my third stanza, is plain enough.

Even so, Aengus and Poor Peter are not the same. We cannot imagine Aengus singing "Tune the Fiddle." Poor Peter has a twinkle; he is audience-aware, he invites the smile and the tear together. These traits give him a place in the world we know, as well as the world of dreams.

Poor Peter
2005

Where Is My Lady?

Where is my lady, O where has she gone?
Over the moonrise and over the dawn.
Follow her easterly, follow the trace
Of her toe on the wind; she has run to the place
Where the morning begins, and the sea and the sky;
Beauty and grace she is, beauty and grace
Hang in the air like chimes where she goes by.

What if I follow, as best I can try,
And ring the wide world, and yet fail in the chase?
Follow her southerly, follow the mark
Of her foot in the light, of her foot in the dark,
Easterly, southerly, follow the train
Where she runs in the starlight, she runs in the rain,
In footfall and starfall, again and again,
Beauty and grace she is, beauty and grace
Hang in the air like chimes where she goes by.

Tune the Fiddle

Tune the fiddle and fetch the drum,
Stamp and clap as the dancers come,
In green and blues, in ranks and queues,
Two by twos in dancing shoes.

Carve the roast and fill the bowl,
Here's to our host, and the thirsty soul,
And the company whole.

O Master of Revels, O Lord of Misrule,
You have set us to school with the ape and the fool!

If we drink, we are giddy, if not, we are dry,
Then let it go by, with never a why.

Up to your toes, Miss Gillian,
Follow your nose, Maid Allison,
Watch how she goes, Dame Jocelyn,
One, two, three, A, B, C, merrily.

Dance to the cembalo, dance to the pipe,
Step to the measure while beauty is ripe,
The lad and the lass and the music will pass,
As the wine from the glass, as the dew from the grass.

Skip and away, young Jeremy,
Best of the day, good Timothy,
What do you say, Squire Anthony,
Four, five, six, candlewicks, fishing sticks.

Ladies fair will dance in the air,
Gallants tall will chase them all,
And catch them as they fall.

Tune the fiddle and fetch the drum,
Stamp and clap as the dancers come,
In green and blues, in ranks and queues,
Two by twos in dancing shoes.

The Ballad of Poor Peter

Gentles, children, come awhile
My song to hear,
And if the song be worth a smile,
Or worth a tear,
Then grant Poor Peter but a penny,
Or two or three if you have many,
Or nothing if you haven't any,
And keep good cheer.

Upon a day, along a way,
I met a child.
She said, "Come find me if you can;
You lost me when the world began."
I asked her meaning, but she ran
Into the wild.

Now where she went, and what she meant,
I do not know,
Or how the world was first begun,
But I will find where she has run,
And follow her beyond the sun,
And ask, before the world is done,
How came it so.

And now I pass, a white old man,
From there to here,
By wit and wile,
A skip, a footstep and a year,
A minute and a mile,
To find her where the world began,
And sing of her, as best I can,
And if the song be worth a tear,
Or yet a smile,
Then grant Poor Peter but a penny,
Or two or three if you have many,
Or nothing if you haven't any,
And bless you all the while.

Various Choral Pieces (Album Notes)*

All the poets represented are old favorites of mine. Keats heads my pantheon, with Masefield a close second. I would choose the same two, in the same order, for comic poetry. Keats' "There Was a Naughty Boy" is a delicious example. In Masefield's "Ballet Russe," a ballerina dances to a Chopin piano accompaniment. My setting aims for tunes Chopin might have written but didn't. Although this text and my "Beauty Come Dancing" scan in iambic pentameter, I set both to waltzes to highlight the dance theme. That can be tricky.

E.A. Robinson, like Masefield, paid no court to modernism. "For a Dead Lady" and "Eros Tyrannos" build like Bach fugues. Few can match him for cadence and the longer breath. The fateful anapests of "The Destruction of Sennacherib" put Byron among those few. Sara Teasdale's "Those Who Love the Most" shows the equal power of a lighter touch.

"Shenandoah" has haunted me since I first heard it sung by Fred Waring's Pennsylvanians nearly eighty years ago. My arrangement pays tribute to what I remember of his. In my setting of "La Belle Dame sans Merci," a clarinet sings what a bird would have sung in that birdless and desolate place.

That poem offers a composer a natural climax building to the line "Thee hath in thrall" in the elfin grot. My own "The Old Man in the Night," more than twice as long, is reflective throughout and really has no climax at all. I contrived two anyhow, as music of this length tends to need them, in the parts beginning "It was here I sought the night" and "O Beautiful my Love." When we recorded it near Amsterdam, along with the other choruses, I realized that I had botched the orchestration of that first climax. I rewrote it. Luckily, James Gaffigan and the chorus and orchestra were available for a patch session two months later, with me listening in from California. Another narrow escape!

---

*These composer's notes were written for the recording *Beauty Come Dancing*, an album of choral settings of poems by Masefield, Keats, Teasdale, Robinson, Byron and Dowson, as well as "The Old Man in the Night" and the three poems by myself directly following.

Anna Pavlova in the Ballet Sylphyde • Valentin Serov

Beauty Come Dancing
2013

Beauty come dancing, beauty come apace,
Beauty and spring are full, come dancing lest
They lapse unharvested, the hour is pressed,
Diana's hounds are gathered for the chase,
Orion puts his shoulder to the trace,
And drives the stars to pasture in the west.

Where will the lapwing go, and where the lawn?
Over to windward, over and away,
Too soon the curfew sounds, too soon we pay
Passage to where the seeps of time are drawn,
Song ends, the dancer curtseys, all is gone
To mist and mystery and yesterday.

Beauty come dancing now, the world is young,
Set foot upon the springtime, all the world
Is loud with music; mirth and music spill
And set the sky to dancing, rung by rung
Stars in their lattice dance to music sung
By owl and cricket, jar and whippoorwill.

The Old Man in the Morning
2013

Here where she walked, her children's children play,
It is all spring, all morning, just as then,
Fennel and fern and springtime come again,
But she brought beauty to another day.
We cannot hold the robin or the rose,
Here where she walked and spoke, another goes,
And she borne westward, westward and away.

Here where she walks, her foot, her hair, her hand,
She is all rose and lily, red and white,
She is the morning, she and all the land
Are new again, awoken from the night,
All new, all found, the cloves of Samarkand,
The hawks of Ida calling at the height.

Shenandoah
Adapted from the traditional song
2015

Most of my contribution to this text was in choosing among lines and stanzas already published. I also substituted "I hear her voice across the water" from published alternatives in the third stanza.

Oh Shenandoah, I long to see you,
Away, you rolling river.
Oh Shenandoah, I long to hear you,
Away, I'm bound away, across the wide Missouri.

Missouri, she's a mighty river,
Hi-o, you rolling river.
When she rolls down, her topsails shiver,
Away, I'm bound away, across the wide Missouri.

Oh Shenandoah, I love your daughter,
Away, you rolling river.
I hear her voice across the water,
Away, I'm bound away, across the wide Missouri.

For sev'n long years I've heard her calling,
Away, you rolling river.
For sev'n long years I've heard her calling,
Away, I'm bound away, across the wide Missouri.

Photo by David Graham / EyeEm / Getty Images

Children by the Christmas Tree • Leopold Graf von Kalckreuth

Four Christmas Carols (Program Notes)

In all these Christmas carols, I wrote the music first, and then found words to fit. This explains why some lines in the last two carols don't scan as we would otherwise expect them to; the melody tended to dictate the number of syllables and the placement of accents. *Prima la musica, e poi le parole!*

Four Christmas Carols
2011

Call the Children
(English verse by Gordon Getty, Latin from Vespers service for Christmas Day, antiphon to the Magnificat)

Hodie Christus natus est, noe!
Hodie Salvator apparuit, alleluia!
Hodie in terra canunt angeli, noe!

Call the children, near and far,
Take them where the Maiden sings,
Where the gifts and candles are,
Show the baby from the star,
The shepherds and the kings.

Hodie laetantur archangeli, noe!

Call the creatures, far and near,
Side by side they come to hear
The song she sings him; wolf and sheep,
Fox and foal together keep,
The leopard and the deer.

Hodie exultant justi, dicentes:
Gloria in excelsis Deo, alleluia, noe!

She sings of what the creatures know,
Of what the birds and children say,
Of whence we came and where we go,
Until she folds the night away
For Christmas Day.

The Snow Child

Where is the child that will come in the snow?
Go where the winds and the caravans go.
Follow the star path to see where it brings,
Angels and farriers, shepherds and kings.

Weave Him a coverlet, weave Him a gown
Velvet and gossamer, flannel and down,
Weave Him a diadem, laurel and thorn,
Gifts for the child in the snow newly born.
Maiden and nightingale sing Him to sleep.
Now all together lie, shepherd and sheep.
Music will stay with Him all the night long,
Music again when they waken in song.

Run to the Window

Listen! Run to the window,
Here in the starlight, shining all night long.
Ladies, nobles and gentry,
Run to the window, hear our Christmas song.

Snowfall, here in the starlight,
Cedar and aspen wear a silver comb.
Children, where does the night go?
Off to the westland, where the stars come home.

Once where a star came
Three kings rode a-following,
Off to the westland by day and by night,
All through the day and night.

Snowfield, white in the starlight,
Mountain and meadow wear a bridal gown.
Children, where does the world go?
Off to a dreamland as the snow comes down.

Sing a song of Christmas,
Christmas in the forest,
Christmas song and Christmas laughter,
Christmas here and Christmas after.

Snowfall, mountain and meadow,
Cedar and aspen wear a silver cloak.
Bless you, high in the window,
Bless us together, goodly gentlefolk.

Once in dreamland
A maid sang a lullaby,
Horses held watch and three kings knelt beside,
Knelt by her side.

Children, where does the wind blow,
Where does the world go, and our Christmas song?
Tell us, here in the starlight,
Here in the snowfield, snowing all night long.

Candles on the Tree

Candles on the tree and the guests come calling,
Children at the window and the snowflakes falling,
Mittens from the sleigh ride,
Warming by the fireside,
Merry, merry Yuletide, everyone good …

Father, carve the goose, Mother, bring the brandy,
Suzie, fetch the licorice and sugar candy,
Jenny, get the pastries,
Molly, get the cream cheese,
Buttermilk and chickpeas,
Gingerbread and dainties,
Someone find the mint, please, everyone good …

Billy does a jig on the pickle barrel,
Auntie, lead the table in a Christmas carol,

Julie, hunt the slipper,
Bob and Sally with her,
All of us together, everyone good ...

Granny, sing a tune, Father, tell a story,
Parson, play the fiddle as we toast Old Glory,
Here's to all the Irish,
Pelicans and catfish,
Onions and the soapdish,
Anything outlandish,
Heartily we all wish everyone good ...

Now the room is dark and the embers glowing,
Presents piled and waiting and the window showing
Just a hint of dawn peep,
Children down the stairs creep,
Daddy, Mommy, come, keep Christmas morning,
Daddy, Mommy, Daddy, Mommy, Mommy, hurry, Daddy, hurry,
Merry Christmas, all of us and everyone,
Good cheer!

Gretchen to Faust (Program Notes)

I read Goethe's *Faust* in spring 2015. I was bowled over by the prison scene that ends Part I. I wrote the verse for *Gretchen to Faust* a little later, adapting some of Goethe's lines and adding my own. To him I owe "Tomorrow would have been my wedding day." She asks to bury them: "My mother in the best place … My brother by her side, and then myself / A little way apart, but not too far." The last line is such a masterstroke that I found a way to steal it twice.

Gretchen to Faust
Adapted from Goethe by Gordon Getty
2015

You should not stay, for we are shadows here,
My mother and my brother and my child,
And I, and there are voices in the dark
And darker things, and angels too, who hold
Their eyes because my baby had no name,
Because I did a dark thing, and because
Tomorrow would have been my wedding day.

But that was once, and now the time has come
For you to find a place to bury us,
My mother in the best place, where the sun
Comes earliest, a place of lilies, where
Birdsong and windsong come to comfort her,
And brook song down below, and cricket song,
My brother by her side, and then myself
A little way apart, but not too far,
My baby at my breast.

                Then you must go
Into the world, and do great things, and build,
And teach, and mend the world, and find a home,
And give a child a name,

                              and we will wait,
And stars will watch on us, and angels too,
And brook and birds and lilies and the sky,
Until my mother sings the stars to sleep
And calls my brother home, and calls me too,
A little way apart, but not too far,
And I will see my little child again.

Mephistopheles to Faust (Program Notes)

My first line and a half translate Goethe more or less. The rest is improvised. Faithfulness to Goethe was not a high priority. His prologue in heaven shows that God sees Mephistopheles as a sleazy con artist. I picture him as believing every word he says. He says and believes that he upholds the true faith. He rises to fortissimo in righteous indignation. Light and the world are defilement of the mother darkness that once was all, and will be all again.

Mephistopheles to Faust
Adapted from Goethe by Gordon Getty
2015

I am a part of that which once was all,
The mother darkness before light was born
And shape and breath and destiny, before
The Word ordained the courses of the stars,
Ordained the law, ordained the forfeiture,
Defiance and defilement of the way
Which once was all, and will be all again
When shape and breath and stars and destiny
Lapse in the mother stillness. I am he
Who held and holds to that more ancient faith,
And teaches those who seek.

Old Man on Snowy Road • Sandra Cunningham / Trevillion Images

The Old Man in the Snow (Program Notes)

As of April 2024, this is my most recent poem. It seems that I write verse much less easily than music. It comes fast when once it gets started, but somehow has to build up first from seeds inside. Here the seeds were the phrases "she is the child of beauty," "she is the child of sorrow," and "O beauty broken." They had been with me for a couple of years, I think, in search of a context, when I finally sat down to write the poem on Christmas vacation in Hawaii.

The Old Man in the Snow
In Memoriam
2020

I saw him once again. It was the white
Of winter, all white everywhere, all new,
The world of old rechristened in a hush
Of snowfall. Once again it seemed that he
Had found a place remembered, kept aside,
A special place where she of long ago,
Forever lost, forever held, had passed,
And once again he mused aloud. He said:

"She is the child of beauty, and she sings
What beauty sings, what willow and the thrush
And river sing, of what comes first and last,
Of air and earth and fire and water, things
All of a piece, unmingled, sure and true,
Kept each by each the same, and even so,
Of what all weave together, of the thread
That ties Uranus to his mortal bride,
Of beauty wrought when air and fire decree
Shadows of cloud banks in the westward light,
When air and earth and fire and water cast
Rainfall and rainbow, dusk and eventide,
Moonrise, a rush of wind, a rush of wings,
A star, a rush of stars, the mother night."

He paused. Again I could not leave unheard;
The snow had hardened. Best to wait him through,
Just as before. Now she of memory
Would live in mine as well, for best or worst,
A while at least, and in the thoughts of those
Who hear me. Somewhere now, far off, there rose
Voices, a dog barking, laughter. Then
He spoke once more, and in a softer key:

"She is the child of sorrow, and she knows
What sorrow knows, how one by one we first
Draw hither, one by one we choose, and reach
A hand to take a hand; we speak a word,
Then one by one must pass to whence we drew
And leave the rest in rue for what had been,
What we who knew and saw may stay to teach
To strangers in the speech and song of men.

O beauty broken, beauty taken, shorn,
Gone to the place where world and night began,
Whence beauty drew when first the world was born,
Where go the wind and snow and thrush and man
While we are left to sing and speak and mourn
And hold a name in honor while we can."

AUTHOR'S NOTES ON THE FOUR LIBRETTI

All my libretti draw from classics. My first opera, *Plump Jack*, for example, follows the story of Falstaff and Prince Hal in Shakespeare's *Henry IV*, both parts, and *Henry V*. Then *Usher House*, *The Canterville Ghost* and *Goodbye, Mr. Chips* were adapted from short stories or novellas by Poe, Wilde and James Hilton. All libretti quote those sources in varying degrees. In this book, I show verbatim or near-verbatim quotes by a vertical line at the left of the passage. A dotted line shows approximate quotes. Footnotes will help clarify.

My libretti are mostly prose, not verse. All are meant to work as plays. Prose does not lend itself to vocal melodies as easily as verse. So my usual style in setting them has meant keeping the melodies in the accompaniment, even in arias, except when I switch from prose to verse as at the end of *The Canterville Ghost*. And setting prose can bring problems in rhythm as well as melody. Many times, in my libretti, I have tweaked the original for no reason but to keep the rhythmic flow.

This explains some of the cases where Shakespeare or Poe or Wilde or Hilton say one thing, and I turn it into something different. It doesn't explain all of them. For reasons both practical and artistic, opera must consolidate and condense. Sung lines move slower than spoken ones. Opera must tell the story in fewer words, and usually with fewer characters to allow the audience enough time to know each better. I merge some characters and scenes, and leave out others, to keep within that budget.

In my libretto to *Plump Jack*, for example, I sometimes consolidate by giving Shakespeare's lines to characters other than those he named. Thus I leave Poins out, and make Boy, rather than Poins, Hal's sidekick and confidante. Likewise I enlarge Davy's role by giving him Silence's lines and songs in the Pistol's News scene. In such cases, I show Shakespeare's original choice in parentheses after mine.

My libretto to *Goodbye, Mr. Chips* expands Doctor Merrivale's role by making him the narrator who keeps the audience abreast of the flashbacks and flash-forwards. Where he is shown as quoting from the source, that means that he is quoting from Hilton's narrative, and in one case from a line given to Rivers in the novel.

In the end, we composers and librettists cannot fully account for our decisions. We try to consider everything, and then choose from the gut. When composer and librettist are the same, as with me, at least we have no one to blame but ourselves when results go wrong.

PLUMP JACK

Jolly Jack Falstaff, King Henry IV, Part 1, Act II, Sc. 4, unknown artist, Lebrecht Music & Arts/Alamy Stock Photo

Plump Jack (Program Notes)

A wise scholar has said that the real protagonist in the plays from which *Plump Jack* is drawn is neither Hal nor Falstaff, but the English people. We see an age in which war, peril and treason crowd everywhere, but in which spite and malaise cannot be imagined. There are no villains in the three plays, and scarcely an unsympathetic character.

A chief theme is the conflict between the worlds of impulse and responsibility. Falstaff and Hal are large enough to be at home in both, but must take the main roles in the struggle between them. In the end, Shakespeare endorses both worlds and both men, and so should we. We are meant to love Falstaff, and yet support every word of Hal's renunciation of him. Whether we humanly can do both these things has been much debated, but there is little doubt that Shakespeare intended us to. Falstaff has just closed the preceding scene, when he has learned of the old king's death, with the words "Let us take any man's horses; the laws of England are at my commandment! Blessed be those that have been my friends, and woe to my Lord Chief Justice!" Shakespeare may be preparing us for the banishment that will follow. It may also be relevant that the defeat of the Armada was of very recent memory when the three plays were written, and that English audiences might have been willing then to give old friends' feelings a low priority against the soundness of the state.

And soundness of the state is the real issue in Falstaff's banishment, rather than any hollow "confirmation conversion" of Hal to establishment mores. Shakespeare takes pains to reassure us of this. Hal's wooing of Katherine in *Henry V* will be set in unbuttoned prose, full of humor and self-deprecation. Hal has not lost the common touch. He is never a prig, but rather always a king who does his duty to old friends and strangers even-handedly.

For Shakespeare's audience, Henry V was one of the greatest Englishmen in history, and the three plays are built around this perception. Never mind that historians today take a dimmer view of him. What matters is that the plays and *Plump Jack* can't work if Hal loses our respect at any point, particularly in the banishment scene. He will lose it if he pulls his punches there. He must chill Falstaff to the bone without the least indication that he either enjoys the business or is squeamish about it. In particular, he must not smile. He must leave the crowd desperately glad they are not Falstaff, and convinced that they have a great and fair king. No doubt the scene plays easier, in an antiheroic age, if Hal is shown as a demagogue whose latent mean streak has been brought out by power. But it cheats Shakespeare, and it cheats the audience in the end.

The court scenes are all gravity and melancholy, while the scenes in Eastcheap and Gloucestershire are all zest and sunshine. Stanislavsky must be forgotten when we enact the latter. The Falstaffian men are built on familiar theatrical models, but exalted and ennobled by genius. Pistol is the *miles gloriosus* (glorious soldier) of Roman comedy, the grandiloquent blowhard who would not frighten a moth. Think of Yosemite Sam. Better still, see Robert Newton's Pistol in Olivier's movie of *Henry V*. Shallow is the soul of Merry England, the irrepressible opposite of Pistol. Think of Mr. Magoo.

Hostess has more dimension. By giving her some lines of Doll Tearsheet, I have cobbled together a romantic history and love duet between Hostess and Falstaff which does not exist in the plays. She can be as shrill as a fishwife in firing up the constables, and then otherworldly in recollecting moments of tenderness. Hostess and Shallow must draw tears as well as laughter.

Falstaff is all the world. We meet him at the top of his game; outwitting his arresters, winning the crowd, pulling the Chief Justice's beard and borrowing another ten pounds, under his nose, for good measure. His next scene at Gad's Hill is the endearing opposite. Here Falstaff is flustered, flummoxed and apoplectic as Hal and Boy play their tricks on him. It makes little difference whether Falstaff is really fooled or is pretending, since the scene plays and registers about the same either way. It is at Gad's Hill that we love Falstaff most.

Love him we must, since all who know him do. He is mourned in the end as much as Hamlet or Brutus or Lear. "He's in Arthur's bosom," says Hostess, even though she never saw a farthing back from him. Bardolph adds the most beautiful tribute of all: "Would I were with him, wheresome'er he is, either in heaven or in hell." (I give the line to all of the Falstaffians.) Before Shakespeare invented Falstaff, the world was not accustomed to comic figures who aroused feelings of that kind. A great performer can show us why this one does.

Origins of *Plump Jack*

The three plays of Henry IV and V add literary invention to famous history. This rooting in fact, as with *Julius Caesar,* seems to give them a head start toward a story line more plausible and vital than what we expect from the time. I found them an easy choice when Sam Wannamaker suggested in 1982 that I should set something by Shakespeare. The opera grew by pieces. A part of what is now the Boar's Head Inn scene was performed by John Del Carlo and Paul Sperry and the San Francisco Symphony in 1985. Within two years I had added "Shallow's Orchard," "Banishment" and "Off to War," and all four scenes were performed by the same forces with added singers and chorus. I then filled out the story with spoken scenes, changing Shakespeare as little as possible, and gradually set those spoken scenes to music as I came to realize that I could not control moods and inflections in any other way.

Mood and inflection are everything in *Plump Jack*. The words come first, and I prefer them to keep the contours and cadences of the spoken stage. Shakespeare in any case is mainly prose and iambic pentameter, both of which I tend to hear as recitative. Thus I place most of the musical content in the orchestra, like Wagner in *The Ring*, and fit a recitative-like prosody to this melodic background. Most of the few vocal melodies, such as the choruses in "Jerusalem" and "Off to War," are set to my own texts, or to other verse of Shakespeare's time. His drinking songs in "Pistol's News" scan in tetrameter, however, and are composed melodically.

This bias toward recitative, leaving most melody to the accompaniment, makes it easy to write *ossias* to suit voices of different ranges. I need only pick other notes in the harmonies in a sequence that keeps the rough shape of the line. Thus Falstaff may be sung by bass-baritone or high baritone, and Henry IV by bass-baritone or bass. A single bass-baritone might therefore double both roles, following Peter Sellars' fine idea, although singing Falstaff alone is an ample workload.

Taking my cue from the plays, I wanted *Plump Jack* to be bursting at the seams, as vivid and varied and multitudinous as possible. I could not have done that within the musical idioms of Shakespeare's time, even if I wanted to try, and like other composers I am pretty much stuck with my own musical language anyhow. But I have sought realism by quoting music from the Renaissance wherever I usefully could. Falstaff's reference to the "Carman's

Whistle" in "Shallow's Orchard," for example, is set to that once-popular tune. Students will also recognize "Tapster, Drinker" in the first bars of "Pistol's News," and again whenever Davy is about to sing. Other quotations include the "Agincourt Song" and "L'Homme Armé" (both twice) in "Off to War," and the Second Agincourt Song ("Enforce we us") in "Banishment." The longest and most interesting quotations are also in "Banishment," in the offstage Latin plainsong that begins and ends this scene. These are apparently the actual words and music sung at the coronation of Henry V, beginning with the Proper Mass for that week ("*Judica me Deus* …") and ending with the Ordinary Mass ("*Agnus Dei*").

I would have stolen more if I had found more worth stealing. I set "Veni, Sancte Spiritus," in the "Jerusalem" scene, in a way to suggest a work of the time because I could not find an authentic setting that I liked. Authenticity does not imply quality. Likewise the "bagpipe" music from "Off to War" (oboes and strings *non vibrato*), and the woodwind motifs from that scene, suggest the period within my own notions of how such music ought to go. Many touches in *Plump Jack* are meant to give an impression of Ars Nova or earlier schools without fooling any experts. What matters is that the music must be my best.

Although *Plump Jack* has been performed over the years, or as much of it as existed at a given time, all of it is recently revised. Its slow genesis has tracked my slow development as an orchestrator. Composing and orchestration are separate gifts. Composing is melody, rhythm, harmony and counterpoint. Orchestration is choice of instruments to play notes already written. Composing is like writing a play, and orchestration is like casting the play. Although composing always came easily to me, it has taken good teaching and stubborn repetition to pound orchestration into my head. Good orchestration simply means getting the balances and colors you meant. I preferred to make my own mistakes, rather than let specialists do the orchestration, because the specialists might not know what I meant. At long last, somehow, what I hear back is converging to what was in my mind.

I find it much easier to rank my favorite composers, past and present, than to figure out which ones have influenced my music. It takes shape, and I write it down. Of course it is derivative. I did not invent the triad or the diatonic scale. Beyond that, I am something like an unwed mother who cannot name the father. The composers I most revere begin with Bach, Beethoven,

Schubert and Wagner. Yet I hear little trace of them in *Plump Jack*. What I hear more of, come to think of it, is movie music. Falstaff's monologue in "Gad's Hill" may derive from what we hear when Sylvester is sneaking up on Tweetie Pie. Likewise the harp/violins *ostinato* in Hal's "Banishment" aria, as gentle as the ticking of a time bomb, or the celesta theme that introduces and describes the pilgrims in "Gad's Hill," might fit the same moments in a film where the lines are spoken rather than sung. Movies, after all, are spoken operas where the score tells us what to expect and how things feel.

Movie music is all-inclusive. We might hear heavy metal as the camera tools along the freeway, then Vivaldi for a picnic in the park, then atonalism as the murderer stalks his prey. By the same token, movie music is less proprietary and single-authored than opera. A film score might include nothing original, and no two pieces by the same composer. *Plump Jack* doesn't fit that model, but shows a similar bent in its eclecticism and love of contrasts. Clearly it derives from Western music as a whole, but perhaps from nothing more specific. The surprise is that I myself do not know what my sources are, even though it is my job to study such things.

"Portrait of my Father as a Tarot Card" (2010). Oil on linen. 31" x 41" © Kendalle Getty

Plump Jack (Synopsis)

ACT I

Scene 1: "The Warrant"

Hostess Nell Quickly has summoned Constables Fang and Snare to arrest Falstaff for nonpayment of debt. They do so as he arrives with his entourage, including Pistol, Bardolph and Boy. The Falstaffians fight the constables. The Chief Justice and his men arrive to restore order. A crowd gathers. The Chief Justice chides Falstaff for draft-dodging in the current war with the Scots and Welsh. Hostess explains her grievances to the Chief Justice. Falstaff promises to pay, but inveigles her into dropping the lawsuit and lending him another ten pounds. All leave but Falstaff.

Prince Hal has been watching Falstaff's performance from the crowd, and now comes forward to applaud his audacity. Boy reappears, and reports that pilgrims with fat purses will be crossing Gad's Hill the following morning before daylight. Falstaff plans a robbery and invites Hal to take part. Hal refuses. Boy offers to persuade Hal in private. Falstaff exits. Boy tells Hal of his plot to rob the Falstaffians after they rob the pilgrims, who will actually be Hal's men in disguise. Hal accepts.

Scene 2: "Hal's Memory"

Hal is alone with his memories. He recalls a chiding by his father, King Henry IV, warning him against his life of indolence and folly. He is touched to the heart, and promises to reform.

Scene 3: "Gad's Hill"

We are at Gad's Hill. It is pitch dark. Falstaff cannot find Hal or Boy or his horse, and rails against the ingratitude of man. The others appear and report that the rich pilgrims are about to arrive. All hide. The "pilgrims" (two of Hal's men) trudge in with a moneybag. Falstaff, Pistol and Bardolph attack them and follow them offstage. They reappear with Falstaff holding the supposed loot. Disguised, Hal and Boy enter and drive them off, with

Falstaff losing his plumed hat. Hal and Boy take the moneybag and the hat, and make merry as Falstaff roars in the distance.

Scene 4: "Clarence"

Henry IV and the Chief Justice are discussing the wars at Windsor Palace. Enter Hal's younger brother Thomas of Clarence. Henry IV advises him to stay close to Hal as a moderating influence, and to bear his humors with patience. The king learns that Hal is dining with Falstaff, and laments the fate of his kingdom under the madcap reign to come: "O thou wilt be a wilderness again, / Peopled with wolves, thy old inhabitants."

Scene 5: "Boar's Head Inn"

We are at the Boar's Head Inn. Hal relaxes at his ease. Boy and Hostess Quickly serve him. Falstaff, Pistol and Bardolph enter, flummoxed and bedraggled. Falstaff denounces Hal for his nonappearance at the robbery. He reports his own heroic defense against troops of assailants, the number increasing with each breath. Pistol and Bardolph swear to every word. They turn to see Hal in the disguise he wore at Gad's Hill, twirling Falstaff's plumed hat on his sword, as the "pilgrims" reprise their roles. Falstaff swears that he saw through the trick from the start, and spared Hal's life out of civic duty. Changing the subject, Falstaff invites Hal to rehearse the defense of his playboy lifestyle that he will present to his father. Hal agrees.

The Falstaffians put a stool on the table and heave Falstaff onto it. Playing Henry IV, he denounces Hal and vilifies all his companions save for that single paragon Falstaff. Then the two switch places as Hal plays the father and Falstaff the son. This time the son is flayed for consorting with Falstaff, "that old white-bearded Satan." Falstaff answers "No, my good lord. Banish Pistol, banish Bardolph, banish Boy, banish Nell, but for good Jack Falstaff, kind Jack Falstaff, sweet Jack Falstaff, valiant Jack Falstaff, and therefore more valiant, being, as he is, old Jack Falstaff, banish not him thy Harry's company, banish not him thy Harry's company. Banish Plump Jack, and banish all the world." Hal answers softly, "I do, I will."

Constables bang at the door, demanding that Falstaff join in the wars. All exit but Falstaff and Hostess. These two have known each other "some twenty-nine years come peascod-time," through thick and thin, and share a tender moment before he emerges to face down the constables and march off to war.

ACT II

Scene 1: "Shallow's Orchard"

We are in Justice Shallow's orchard in Gloucestershire. Enter Falstaff, Bardolph, Boy and Shallow. Falstaff and Shallow reminisce about merriment and wenching in times long gone. Shallow leaves to organize dinner for the Falstaffians. Bardolph and Boy follow. Falstaff, alone, lampoons Shallow and declares a plan to swindle him.

Scene 2: "Jerusalem"

Henry IV confers with his council at Westminster. Warwick enters with the news that the rebellion against him has been crushed. In the rejoicing the king falls ill. Hal enters, repents his follies, and is reconciled with his dying father.

Scene 3: "Davy's Ledger"

Shallow, in his sumptuous country drawing room, cannot find the silver and cloth he needs to impress his dinner guests. He climbs to a high cupboard and tumbles head over heels. His snooty and super-efficient steward Davy appears with servants. Without a word, Davy restores order, finds the missing tableware in the chest on which Shallow had balanced in his climb, and directs setting of the table. Shallow, sunny and unflusterable, discusses farm matters with Davy as if nothing had gone awry. Davy is instructed to treat Falstaff well: "A friend in the court is better than a penny in purse." Falstaff and his men enter and are ushered to the table. Again Falstaff tarries to tell us his designs on Shallow. Meanwhile Davy, out of their sight, takes a nip from the wine flask.

Scene 4: "Pistol's News"

At Shallow's table, all are four sheets to the wind. Davy, insufferable when sober, is the life of the party when drunk. He sings bawdy songs as he pours, and all join in. As he finally collapses, Pistol is announced with news from London. The news, decoded with effort by Falstaff, is that Henry IV is dead and Hal is now king. Elated, Falstaff makes plans to share the spoils and to settle accounts with the Chief Justice.

Scene 5: "Banishment"

A crowd including the Falstaffians and Shallow gathers along the route of Henry V's coronation procession. Falstaff has "borrowed" a thousand pounds from Shallow, supposedly to arrange Shallow's political advancement. The king's train approaches. As all others kneel, Falstaff runs into the road to embrace his old chum. The king stares him down, blisters him and banishes him "not to come near our person by ten mile." The procession continues with Falstaff prostrate. Shallow and the Falstaffians stay. Falstaff pulls himself up and laughs off the tongue-lashing as public relations. Certainly Shallow cannot have his money back, or even half; it will still buy him great office as originally bargained. "I shall be sent for in private to him," swears Falstaff as he leads them off. "I shall be sent for soon at night!" Snow falls on the empty street as monks offstage sing the Agnus Dei.

Scene 6: "Muse of Fire"

Cannon are heard in the darkness. Unseen voices sing of preparations for war with France. They also tell us that Pistol and Hostess are married. A spotlight finds Boy asking these two to come to Falstaff, who is very sick. All add, "The king hath killed his heart." Blackout and cannon again as the king exhorts the nation to war. Once more the spotlight finds Hostess calling the Falstaffians to their dying master.

Scene 7: "Off to War"

It is just before dawn outside the Boar's Head Inn. Pistol calls out to Bardolph and Boy, and tells them Falstaff is dead. Hostess describes his death. As dawn breaks, the street fills with men to go to war and women to see them off. Recruiting officers, vendors, tumblers, street entertainers and pipers join the scene. Companies march off as others form. The king and his train pass. Finally Pistol, Bardolph and Boy march away. Hostess and the women remain to bid their men farewell.

PLUMP JACK
Opera in Two Acts

Libretto
By Gordon Getty
1985

Adapted from Shakespeare's *Henry IV, Parts One and Two,* and *Henry V*

Cast of Characters in Order of Appearance

HOSTESS (Nell Quickly), keeper of Boar's Head Inn
FANG, Sergeant
SNARE, Yeoman
Sir John FALSTAFF
PISTOL, member of Falstaff's retinue
BARDOLPH, member of Falstaff's retinue
CHIEF JUSTICE
HAL, Prince of Wales (later Henry V)
BOY, Falstaff's squire
HENRY IV
FIRST "PILGRIM"
SECOND "PILGRIM"
Thomas of CLARENCE, Hal's younger brother
FIRST CAPTAIN
SECOND CAPTAIN
Robert SHALLOW
Earl of WARWICK
DAVY, Shallow's head butler
Townspeople, Constables, Chief Justice's men, Guests at the inn, Chorus of monks, Shallow's servants, Lords of parliament, Soldiers

NOTE: Text with a solid line in the left margin indicates original source material. Text with a dot in the left margin indicates adapted source material.

ACT I

Act 1, Scene 1 *"The Warrant"* (From H IV 2, 2, 1; H IV 1, 1, 2 and H IV 2, 2, 4)

A square in London, about noon. A sign on a building in the foreground shows a boar's head. A few drunks sleep in doorways. A fruit vendor dozes at his stand. After a few seconds of this tableau, Hostess, Fang and six to ten constables rush in. These men are zealous but brainless, Elizabethan Keystone Kops.

HOSTESS
Master Fang, have you entered the action?

CONSTABLES
Have you, have you?

FANG
Hostess Nell Quickly, …

CONSTABLES
What?

FANG
… it is entered.

CONSTABLES
Good!

FANG
Here is the warrant.

CONSTABLES
Show us! Show us!

HOSTESS
Where's your yeoman?

CONSTABLES
Yeoman!

HOSTESS[1]
Is he a lusty yeoman?

CONSTABLES
Yeoman!

HOSTESS[2]
Will he stand fast?

FANG
(*To one of the constables*) Sirrah, where's Snare?

CONSTABLES
Snare!

HOSTESS
O, Lord, ay, good Master Snare!

Snare runs in, trips, and crashes through the fruit stand. Sleepers are jarred awake. Deadpan and lightning quick, Snare and the constables clean up the mess.

FANG
Snare, we must arrest Sir John Falstaff.

Alarm among Snare and constables.

CONSTABLES
Not Falstaff!

SNARE[3]
It may cost us all our lives, for he will stab!

CONSTABLES
Alas the day!

---

[1] "Is't," not "Is he"
[2] "Will a stand to't?" not "Will he stand fast?"
[3] "some of us," not "us all"

Upon a Day | 75

FANG
(*Steps forward, hunching into a wrestling stance.*) If I can close with him, I care not for his thrust!

HOSTESS
(*Joins Fang.*) Nor I, neither! I'll be at your elbow!

SNARE, CONSTABLES (Fang alone in the play)
(*Snare joins them, showing his uppercut.*) If I fist him but once, if he come but within my vice!

Snare and Fang grapple with imaginary Falstaffs. The other constables join in. The imaginary Falstaffs are polished off. Hostess snatches the warrant from Fang and holds it up for all to see.

HOSTESS
(*Holding the warrant under the constables' noses by turn, as if any of them could read*) A hundred marks he owes me, a hundred marks!

SNARE, FANG, CONSTABLES
What? So much!

HOSTESS
And I have borne, and borne, and borne, and been fubbed off, and fubbed off, from this day to that, that it is a shame to be thought on!

SNARE, FANG, CONSTABLES
So much to bear! Such a shame!

HOSTESS
(*Pointing with the warrant*) Yonder he comes, … (*All look. Consternation.*)

SNARE, FANG, CONSTABLES
Men, form ranks! Up truncheons!

The constables form a double line, half kneeling in front and half standing behind.

HOSTESS
… and that malmsey-nose knave, Bardolph, with him, …

SNARE, FANG, CONSTABLES
Hold fast, lads!

HOSTESS[4]
… and that swaggerer, Pistol!

SNARE, FANG, CONSTABLES
Hold, lads!

Enter Falstaff, Pistol, and Bardolph. Falstaff is jovial, nonchalant, as if he didn't see the constables.

FALSTAFF[5]
How now, Nell? Whose mare's dead? What's the matter?

FANG[6]
Sir John, I arrest you at the suit of Hostess Quickly.

FALSTAFF[7]
Draw, Bardolph, Pistol! Throw the jade in the gutter! (*They fight.*)

HOSTESS
Throw me in the gutter! I'll throw thee in the gutter!

SNARE, FANG, CONSTABLES (Fang alone)
Help! A rescue! A rescue!

Enter the Chief Justice and his men. In contrast to Fang's bunch, these are able officers. He is a stern but kindly man with a twinkle in his eye. The combatants freeze. Hostess kneels.

---

4   Shakespeare does not include Pistol in this scene.
5   "Nell" is added.
6   "Mistress," not "Hostess"
7   "channel," not "gutter," and "quean," not "jade." "Pistol" is added.

SNARE[8]
(*Aside to Hostess*) This is the lord that committed the Prince for boxing his ear.

FANG, CONSTABLES
My Lord Chief Justice!

While order is being restored, a crowd gathers. A spotlight finds Hal and Boy joining it. Those about Hal start to kneel or curtsy, but he stops this with a gesture and taps his lips for secrecy. We see at once that he is on easy terms with all of them. Falstaff notices him, and covertly gives him the high sign.

CHIEF JUSTICE[9]
(*Chiding, not menacing*) How now, Sir John? What, are you brawling here? You should have been well on your way to York, in the King's wars. (*To the constables*) Stand from him, fellows. Wherefore hang upon him? (*The constables scurry away from Falstaff.*) Sir John, explain.

As Falstaff is about to begin, Hostess runs in front of him.

HOSTESS[10]
O my most worshipful lord, I am Hostess Nell Quickly, and he is arrested at my suit. He hath eaten me out of house and home. (*Falstaff mimics shoveling it in. Laughter from Boy and the crowd.*) He hath put all my substance into that fat belly of his, and will not pay back a groat! (*Laughter continues.*)

CHIEF JUSTICE
How comes this, Sir John? Again? Mend, mend, Sir John. Have you not misled the youthful Prince? And will you now enforce this poor woman to so rough a course to come into her own? Have you forgotten your years?

BOY, BARDOLPH, PISTOL, CROWD
(*In turns or together, between Chief Justice's lines above; always in merriment*) He'll catch it now! You're right, boy! He'll take a chiding! Guilty as charged! He's got you there! For shame, Sir John! Old John!

---

[8] Adapted from H IV 2,1,2. "nobleman," not "lord."
[9] "in the King's wars" is added.
[10] "a poor widow of Eastcheap," not "Hostess Nell Quickly." "and will not pay back a groat" is added.

The crowd presses forward in anticipation of Falstaff's performance. From now on, Falstaff is playing to them, and particularly to Hal.

BOY
Hear him now!

BARDOLPH, PISTOL, CROWD
(*Puckish, playful*) On your mettle, Sir John!

FALSTAFF[11]
My lord, this is a poor mad soul, (*Boy and Crowd echo Falstaff. Hostess is miffed.*) and she says up and down the town that her eldest son is like you. (*Hal and the crowd crack up. Hostess is fit to be tied.*) Touching my age, I was born three o'clock in the afternoon, with a white beard and something a round belly. (*Crowd mirth again.*) But the truth is, …

BOY, BARDOLPH, PISTOL, CROWD
Tell him, Sir John!

FALSTAFF[12]
… I am only old in judgment and understanding, and he that will caper with me for a thousand pound, (*Slyly, out of the side of his mouth*) let him lend me the money, …

BOY, BARDOLPH, PISTOL, CROWD
He'll never get it back!

FALSTAFF[13]
… and have at him! (*Falstaff grabs a pikestaff from Snare, blocks imaginary blows with it, and then shoves the air with his foot. The crowd cracks up.*) For the box of the ear that the Prince gave you, I have checked him for it, and the young lion repents, …

---

[11] Adapted from H IV 2, 1, 2
[12] Ibid.
[13] Ibid.

BOY, SNARE, FANG, BARDOLPH, PISTOL, CONSTABLES, CROWD
(*Snare, Fang and constables devoutly, but Boy and crowd in fun*) Mea culpa, me absolve.

FALSTAFF[14]
… marry, not in sackcloth, (*Lugubriously, with a broad wink at Hal*) but in sack. (*Hal and the crowd roar with laughter. The audience should sense that neither Hal nor the Chief Justice bears a grudge over the earboxing incident, and that the Chief Justice tolerates Falstaff's impertinence with good grace.*) But, my lord, I say the widow shall have justice.

BARDOLPH, PISTOL, CROWD
Bravo, Sir John! Fun's fun, but fair's fair!

FALSTAFF[15]
Good Mistress Quickly, what is the gross sum that I owe thee?

HOSTESS
(*Reproachfully*) Marry, if thou wert an honest man, thyself and the money too. (*Innocent, otherworldly, lost in memory*) Thou didst swear to me, upon a parcel-gilt goblet, sitting in my Dolphin Chamber, at the round table, by a sea-coal fire, upon Wednesday in Whitsun-week, when the Prince broke thy head for liking his father to a singing man of Windsor. (*Falstaff claps hand to head in mock pain, to the delight of Hal and the crowd.*) Thou didst swear to me then, as I was washing thy wound, to marry me and make me the lady thy wife. Canst thou deny it? (*Falstaff shrugs his shoulders, palms up, in a "What's wrong with that?" gesture. Again the crowd roars with laughter.*) And did not goodwife Keech, the butcher's wife, come in then, and call me Gossip[16] Quickly, telling us she had a good dish of prawns, whereby thou didst desire to eat some, whereby I told thee they were ill for a green wound? (*Falstaff claps hands to stomach, eyes bulging in mock nausea. Hal and the crowd roar again.*) And didst thou not, when she was gone downstairs, desire me to be no more so familiar with such poor people, saying that ere long they should call me madam? (*This time the laughter is faint and uncomfortable.*

---

[14] Ibid.
[15] "Good Mistress Quickly" is added.
[16] "Gossip" meant something like "neighbor," but the modern meaning is funnier here.

Hostess' homely tale has begun to touch the crowd. Some wipe their eyes.) And didst thou not kiss me, and bid me fetch thee thirty shillings? I put thee now to thy book oath. Deny it if thou canst.

Dead silence. The crowd doesn't know whether to laugh or weep.

CHIEF JUSTICE
(*Quietly*) Sir John, pay her the debt.

SNARE, FANG, BARDOLPH, PISTOL, CROWD, CONSTABLES
Pay her, Sir John!

FALSTAFF
(*Feigning indignation, as if no other thought than to pay her had ever entered his mind*) My lord, as I am a gentleman, I shall.

SNARE, FANG, BARDOLPH, PISTOL, CROWD, CONSTABLES
Hurrah, Sir John!

HOSTESS
So you said before.

FALSTAFF
(*Still indignant*) As I am gentleman, every penny.

SNARE, FANG, BARDOLPH, PISTOL, CROWD, CONSTABLES
That's the spirit! Treat her right, Sir John!

BOY
(*Aside to Hal*) Listen now!

FALSTAFF[17]
(*His mood brightens.*) I shall receive money o' Thursday.

BOY
Watch him now!

---

[17] Taken from H IV 2.2.4

FALSTAFF[18]
Thou shalt have a cap tomorrow.

BOY
He's casting his net!

FALSTAFF
Come, no more words of it.

HOSTESS[19]
(*Distraught*) By this heavenly ground I tread on, you'll put me off again! I'll never see a farthing back! I must pawn all my plate and the tapestries of my dining chambers!

She weeps. Falstaff takes her in his arms.

FALSTAFF
Glasses, Nell, glasses is the only drinking. And for thy walls, a pretty slight drollery, or the story of the prodigal, is worth a thousand of these bed-hangings and these fly-bitten tapestries.

BOY
Soon she'll be in his pouch!

FALSTAFF[20]
Lend me ten pound until Thursday. Come, an 'twere not for thy humors, there's not a better wench in England. Come, wash thy face and withdraw the action. Tear up the warrant, and lend me ten pound.

HOSTESS
Faith, Sir John, let it be but twenty nobles. In faith, I am loath to pawn all my plate, so God save me, la!

---

[18] Taken from H IV 2, 2, 4
[19] "you'll ... back" is added.
[20] The first sentence is originally "Let it be ten pound." "draw," not "withdraw." The last sentence is added.

FALSTAFF
(*Feigning exasperation*) Let it alone; I'll make other shift. You'll be a fool still.

BOY
Watch her now!

Falstaff stalks away a few steps. Hostess dries her tears, reflects, and decides.

HOSTESS
Well, you shall have it, though I pawn my gown.

She walks to the dumbfounded Fang, takes the warrant from him, and tears it in pieces.

BOY, SNARE, FANG, BARDOLPH, PISTOL, CROWD, CONSTABLES
Poor, poor Hostess!

Hostess and Falstaff embrace. The Chief Justice smiles in good-natured amusement; he has seen it all before. Exeunt all but Hostess, Falstaff, Bardolph and the retainers.

HOSTESS[21]
I hope you'll come to supper tomorrow night. You'll pay me all together?

FALSTAFF
Will I live? Go with her, boys, hook on, hook on.

Exeunt all but Falstaff and Hal.

HAL[22]
(*Coming forward*) Well played, Sir John Barebone!

FALSTAFF
Hal, good morrow!

---

[21] "tomorrow night" is added.
[22] This and the next few lines are adapted from H IV 1, 2, 4 and H IV 2, 1, 4.

Upon a Day | 83

HAL
How long is it ago, lean Jack, since thou saw'st thine own knee?

FALSTAFF
My own knee? When I was about thy years, Harry, I was not an eagle's talon in the waist; I could have crept into any alderman's thumb ring. A plague of sighing and grief; …

HAL
(*In jest*) Poor Jack!

FALSTAFF
… it blows a man up like a bladder. Hal, there's villainous news about; I must to the wars. If our armies join on a hot day, and I brandish anything but a bottle, I would I might never spit white again. (*Hal breaks up. Enter Boy.*) Boy, come join us!

BOY (Poins)[23]
Brave tidings, your worship! Tomorrow morning, by four o'clock early at Gad's Hill, there are pilgrims going to Canterbury with rich offerings, and traders riding to London with fat purses. You and your men may rob them as secure as sleep.

FALSTAFF
(*Rubbing his hands*) Hal, wilt thou join us?

HAL
(*Laughing*) Who, I rob? I, a thief? Not I, by my faith!

FALSTAFF
There's neither honesty, manhood, nor good fellowship in thee, Hal, nor thou cam'st not of the blood royal, if thou dare'st not stand.

HAL
(*Amused, not offended*) Ho, ho, ho!

---

[23] Taken from H IV 1, 1, 2. The first sentence is added.

BOY (Poins)[24]
Sir John, I prithee leave us alone. I'll convince him.

FALSTAFF
Well, Boy, God give thee the spirit of persuasion, and him the ears of profiting. Farewell, you shall find me in Eastcheap.

HAL[25]
Farewell, thou latter spring!

Exit Falstaff.

BOY (Poins)
(*To Hal*) Now, my good lord, ride with us tomorrow; I have a jest to play. Two of your men can play the pilgrims; Falstaff, Bardolph and Pistol will rob them; we will manage to be out of sight when they do. And when they have the booty, if we do not rob them, cut this head from off my shoulders. They will not know who you are; I have a cloak of Kendal green to mask you. The reward for our trouble will be the uproarious lies Sir John will tell us at supper, how thirty at least he fought with, and in the reproof of this lies the jest.

HAL
Well, then I'll go with thee. Farewell.

BOY (Poins)
Farewell, my lord.

Act 1, Scene 2 *"Hal's Memory"* (From H IV 1, 3, 2)

Exit Boy. The stage darkens. Spotlight on Hal. We hear a hubbub of male voices from the dark, beginning a second or two before the music. Another spotlight finds Henry IV standing behind and above Hal in Hal's memory.

---

[24] "the Prince and me," not "us"
[25] "the," not "thou"

HENRY IV[26]
Lords, give us leave. The Prince of Wales and I
Must have some private conference.

The hubbub dies down to silence.

Harry, son, Thou know'st that Percy and Northumberland,
Douglas, and the Archbishop's Grace of York
Rise to make head against us in the north
And shake the peace and safety of our throne.
But why tell this to thee? For all the world,
As thou art to this hour was Richard once,
When I from France set foot at Ravenspurgh.
The skipping king, he ambled up and down,
Mingled his royalty with capering fools,
And grew companion to the common streets.
And in that very line, Harry, standest thou,
For thou hast lost thy privilege. Not an eye
But is a-weary of thy common sight,
Save mine, which hath desired to see thee more,
Which now doth what I would not have it do,
Make blind itself with foolish tenderness.

Henry IV is moved to tears. Spotlight on Henry IV fades out slowly. Spotlight up on Hal.

HAL[27]
So please your majesty, I would I could
Quit all offences I am charged withal,
But some are true. May these, wherein my youth
Hath faulty wandered and irregular,
Find pardon in my true submission.
I shall hereafter, my thrice-gracious lord,
Be more myself, and will redeem myself.
This in the name of God I promise here.

---

[26] "Harry, son" through "north" is loosely adapted. "Grew a companion," not "And grew companion"

[27] The third line is loosely adapted.

Blackout.

Act 1, Scene 3 *"Gad's Hill"* (From H IV 1, 2, 2)

Gad's Hill, night. A horse neighs. Enter Boy and Hal.

BOY (Poins)
Come, shelter, your highness! I have removed Falstaff's horse, and he frets like a gummed velvet.

HAL
Stand close, Boy!

FALSTAFF[28]
(*Offstage*) Boy! Boy and be hanged! Boy!

HAL
(*Calling merrily*) Peace, ye fat-kidneyed rascal! What a brawling dost thou keep!

FALSTAFF[29]
(*Offstage*) Where's Boy, Hal?

HAL
He's walked up to the top of the hill; I'll go fetch him.

Boy and Hal hide. Enter Falstaff with a lantern.

FALSTAFF[30]
Hal! I am accursed to rob in that thief's company; the rascal hath removed my horse and tied him I know not where. If I travel but four foot further afoot, I shall break my wind. Well I doubt not to die a fair death for all this, if I scape hanging for killing that rogue. I have forsworn his company hourly

---

[28] "Poins," not Boy." Shakespeare does not include Boy in this scene.
[29] Ibid.
[30] Ibid.

these two and twenty years, and yet I am bewitched with the rogue. If the rascal hath not given me medicines to make me love him, I'll be hanged. Boy! Eight yards of uneven ground is threescore and ten miles afoot with me, and the stonyhearted rascals know it well enough. A plague upon it when thieves cannot be true to one another. Whew! A plague upon you all! Give me my horse, you rogues, give me my horse, and be hanged!

Enter Hal.

HAL
Peace, ye fat guts! Lay thine ear close to the ground, and list if thou canst hear the tread of travelers.

FALSTAFF
(*Falstaff complies effortfully.*) Hang thyself in thine own heir-apparent garters! If I be taken, I'll peach for this, and if I have no ballads made on you all, and sung to filthy tunes, let a cup of sack be my poison!
Enter Pistol.

PISTOL (Gadshill)
Stand!

FALSTAFF[31]
(*Aside, struggling to his feet*) So I do, against my will. Pistol, what news?
(*Raising his lantern so that Pistol can recognize them*)

PISTOL
O valiant knight,
Bardolph and I stand guard athwart the road,
As dread as Mars, as fierce as Cerberus,
And ready for great deeds.

Enter Bardolph, running.

BARDOLPH
(*Rapid fire, keeping his voice down*) On with your masks! There's money of the king's coming down the hill. 'Tis going to the king's exchequer.

---

[31] "Gadshill," not "Pistol." Shakespeare does not include Pistol in this scene.

FALSTAFF[32]
(*Under his breath*) Bardolph, ye lie, ye rogue. 'Tis going to the king's tavern!

HAL
You three front them there in the narrow lane. I'll close from behind. Boy, guard the horses.

FALSTAFF
Now, masters, every man to his business.

Exeunt Falstaff, Pistol and Bardolph. Boy emerges from hiding.

HAL (Poins)[33]
Boy, where's my disguise?

BOY (Poins)
Here, my lord, hard by.

Exeunt Hal and Boy.

FIRST "PILGRIM"
(*Offstage*) Come, neighbor. The boy shall lead our horses down the hill. (*Enter the two "pilgrims."*) We'll walk afoot awhile, and ease our legs.

Falstaff, Pistol and Bardolph rush in and set upon the "pilgrims," actually Hal's men in disguise.

FALSTAFF, PISTOL, BARDOLPH[34] (Gadshill alone)
Stand!

"PILGRIMS"
Jesus bless us!

---

[32] "Bardolph" is added.
[33] "Poins," not "Boy"
[34] See footnote 31.

FALSTAFF

Strike! Down with them! Cut the villains' throats! Ah, caterpillars, bacon-fed knaves, they hate us youth! Down with them, fleece them!

In the scuffle, the "pilgrims" tumble offstage. Falstaff, Pistol and Bardolph follow them.

FIRST "PILGRIM"

(*Offstage*) O! We are undone, both we and ours forever!

FALSTAFF

(*Offstage*) What, ye fat chuffs! Young men must live. We'll teach ye, faith!

Enter Hal and Boy with lanterns from the opposite side of the stage. As they speak, Hal puts on his disguise.

HAL[35]

The thieves have bound the true men; now might we rob the thieves. It would be argument for a week, laughter for a month, and a good jest forever. Stand close, I hear them coming.

Exeunt Hal and Boy. Enter Falstaff, Pistol and Bardolph.

FALSTAFF[36]

Come, my masters, let us share, then to horse before day. If the Prince be not an arrant coward, there's no equity stirring; there's no more valour in that Hal than in a wild duck.

Enter Hal, disguised.

HAL

Your money! Villains! (*They fight. Pistol and Bardolph run away. After a blow or two, Falstaff runs also, losing his plumed hat and leaving the booty behind. Hal and Boy collect both.*) Got with much ease!

---

[35] "could thou and I," not "might we"
[36] "Poins," not "Hal"

HAL[37]
Now merrily to horse.
The thieves are scattered and possessed with fear
So strongly that they dare not meet each other;
Each takes his fellow for an officer.
Away, good Boy. Falstaff sweats to death,
And lards the lean earth as he walks along.
Were't not for laughing, I should pity him.

BOY (Poins)
How the fat knight roared!

Lights out as Falstaff roars from offstage.

Act 1, Scene 4 *"Clarence"* (From H IV 2, 4, 4 and H IV 2, 4, 5)

We are at Westminster in the Presence Chamber. Lights up on Henry IV and Chief Justice.

HENRY IV[38]
My Lord Chief Justice,
If God shall please to give successful end
To this debate that bleedeth at our doors,
We will our youth lead on to higher fields,
And draw no swords but in the Holy Land.
Only we want a little personal strength,
And pause us, till these rebels, now afoot,
Come underneath the yoke of government.

CHIEF JUSTICE (Warwick)
Both which we doubt not but your majesty shall soon enjoy.

Exit Chief Justice. Enter Clarence.

---

[37] "Ned," not "Boy"
[38] Shakespeare does not put Chief Justice in this scene. The second line is loosely adapted. The fifth line gives "what are sanctified," not "in the Holy Land."

HENRY IV
Thomas, my son of Clarence, come to my side.

CLARENCE
What would my lord and father?

HENRY IV
Nothing but well to thee, Thomas of Clarence.
How chance thou are not with the prince thy brother?
He loves thee, and thou dost neglect him, Thomas.
Thou hast a better place in his affection
Than all thy brothers. Cherish it, my boy.
He hath a tear for pity, and a hand
Open as day for meeting charity.
Yet notwithstanding, being incensed, he's flint,
As humorous as winter, and as sudden.
Chide him for faults, and do it reverently,
Till that his passions, like a whale on ground,
Confound themselves with working. Learn this, Thomas,
And thou shalt be a shelter to thy friends,
A hoop of gold to bind thy brothers in.

CLARENCE
I shall observe him with all care and love.

HENRY IV
Why art thou not at Windsor with him, Thomas?

CLARENCE
He is not there today. He dines in London.

HENRY IV
And how accompanied? Canst thou tell that?

CLARENCE[39]
With Falstaff and his other followers.

---

[39] Originally "with Poins, and the other his continual followers."

HENRY IV[40]
Most subject is the richest soil to weeds,
And he, the noble image of my youth,
Is overspread with them.
- The blood weeps from my heart when I conceive
- The rotten times that you will look upon
When I am sleeping with my ancestors.
For when his headlong riot hath no curb,
When rage and hot blood are his counsellors,
O, my poor kingdom, sick with civil blows!
O, thou wilt be a wilderness again,
Peopled with wolves, thy old inhabitants.

Blackout.

Boar's Head Tavern. Illustration to Henry IV, Part 1, Act 2, scene 4. Unknown artist, c.1840

---

[40] "When I do shape," not "when I conceive." The final three lines are from H IV 2, 4, 5.

Act 1, Scene 5 *"Boar's Head Inn"* (From H IV 1, 2, 4 and H IV 2, 2, 4)

We are at the Boar's Head Inn in Eastcheap. Boy stands looking out a window near the entrance. Hostess and a crowd jostle quietly for sight lines behind him. Hal is at a table downstage, sprawled out at his ease.

BOY
Here they come!

HAL
Everyone ready!

The crowd, rehearsed, scramble for positions at the table and revel as if they had been there all along. Hostess and boy serve them ale and sack. Enter Falstaff, Bardolph and Pistol, all bedraggled.

HAL (Poins)
(*Nonchalant*) Welcome, Jack. How hast thou been?

BOY, HOSTESS, CROWD
Hello, Sir John!

Hostess leads them to a table downstage next to Hal's.

FALSTAFF[41]
A plague of all cowards, I say! Give me a cup of sack, boy.

HOSTESS, HAL, CROWD
Run, lad.

Boy rushes to comply. General merriment is mimed as Falstaff continues, but Falstaff remains the center of attention.

FALSTAFF
You, Prince of Wales! Are you not a coward? You are straight enough in the shoulders; you care not who sees your back.

---

[41] "rogue," not "boy"

BOY, HOSTESS, CROWD
Brave words, Sir John! The prince will pull your whiskers!

FALSTAFF
(*As mimed merriment continues*) There lives not three good men unhanged in England, and one of them is fat, and grows old.

BOY, HOSTESS, HAL, CROWD
(*All in jest*) How poignant! How piteous!

FALSTAFF[42]
Boy, give me a cup of sack! I am a rogue if I drunk today!

HAL
O villain! Thy lips are scarce wiped since thou drunkest last!

BOY, HOSTESS, CROWD
God's truth, Sir John, you've drained your cup.

FALSTAFF[43]
(*Over the laughter*) All's one for that. A plague of all cowards, still say I. There be three of us, men worthy the name, who have taken a thousand pound this morning.

BOY, HOSTESS, HAL, CROWD (Hal alone)
Where is it, Sir John, where is it?

FALSTAFF[44]
Where is it? Stolen from us it is; a hundred on poor three of us!

HOSTESS, HAL, CROWD
What! A hundred, man?

BOY (Hal)
(*Aside to Hal*) Let him alone; we shall have more anon.

---

[42] "Boy" is added.
[43] "four," not "three"
[44] Ibid.

HOSTESS, CROWD
Then more again!

HAL[45]
Speak, Pistol! How was it?

BOY
This will be good!

PISTOL (Gadshill)[46]
(*Rises, acts it out.*) We gallant three set forth upon some dozen …

FALSTAFF
Pistol, you rogue, there were thirty at least, or else I am a peppercorn!

BOY, HOSTESS, CROWD
At least, at least, at least!

HAL
Bardolph, what then?

BOY, HOSTESS, CROWD
Tell us, Bardolph, tell us!

BARDOLPH (Gadshill)[47]
(*Like Pistol, Bardolph rises to act it out.*) We bound them, and then as we were sharing, some six or seven fresh men set upon us.

FALSTAFF
(*Slamming the table*) Sixty or seventy!

BOY, HAL, CROWD
Eighty or ninety!

BARDOLPH, PISTOL
And then came more of them.

---

[45] "Sirs," not "Pistol"
[46] "four," not "gallant three"
[47] "then" is added.

BOY, HOSTESS, HAL, CROWD
What! Fought you with them all?

FALSTAFF[48]
(*Likewise, rises to act.*) If I fought not with a hundred of them, a hundred misbegotten knaves in Kendal green, …

BOY, HOSTESS, HAL, CROWD
Even more! Such knaves!

FALSTAFF
… I am a bunch of radish!

BOY, HOSTESS, HAL, CROWD
Never!

FALSTAFF
I am a rogue if I were not at half sword with them two hours together. I have escaped by a miracle!

BOY, HOSTESS, HAL, CROWD
Praise be!

FALSTAFF
Thou knowest my swordplay, Hal. They drove at me, and I parried their points thus! (*Shows his swordplay.*)

BOY, HOSTESS, HAL, CROWD
Bravo, bravo, Sir John!

FALSTAFF
I am eight times thrust through the doublet, four through the hose, my buckler cut through and through, my sword hacked like a handsaw. (*As Falstaff sings, Hal and Boy put on the green cloaks they wore at Gad's Hill while the men who played the pilgrims put on the clothes they wore as such. One carries the money bag as before. The four move quietly behind Falstaff.*) And then came

---

[48] Reassembled "fifty," not "a hundred"

fifty more of them, and fifty more, and fifty more of these misbegotten rogues in Kendal …

HAL
(*In the same disguised voice he used at Gad's Hill*) Two hundred fifty, then, was it, Jack?

Falstaff freezes.

FIRST "PILGRIM," SECOND "PILGRIM"
Come, neighbor. The boy will lead the horses down the hill.

Falstaff spins to see Hal, Boy and the "pilgrims." The latter are trudging along with their packs as first seen at Gad's Hill. Hal is twirling Falstaff's plumed hat on his swordpoint. Falstaff spins again to face the audience. He is all consternation, hands to mouth. His face brightens. A thought cloud over his head shows a candle flickering on.

FALSTAFF[49]
By the Lord, I knew ye as well as He that made ye. (*General laughter.*) Was it for me to kill the true prince? Thou know'st I am as valiant as Hercules, but beware instinct. The lion will not touch the true prince; instinct is a great matter. I was now a coward on instinct.

BOY, HOSTESS, HAL, BARDOLPH, PISTOL, CROWD
(*In unison with Falstaff*) On instinct.

HAL
Bravo, Jack!

BOY, HOSTESS, BARDOLPH, PISTOL, CROWD
Well escaped, Sir John. (*Cheers and laughter.*)

FALSTAFF[50]
By the Lord, lad, I am glad I spared your life. (*More laughter.*) Hostess, clap shut the doors!

---

[49] Condensed and reassembled
[50] "lads, I am glad you have the money," and "clap to the doors!"

HAL
Boy, have a look outside.

BOY
I will, my lord.

Exit Boy. Hostess shuts the doors.

FALSTAFF
(*To all present, raising his glass*) Gallants, lads, hearts of gold, all the titles of good fellowship come to you!

HOSTESS, HAL, BARDOLPH, PISTOL, CROWD
(*Raising glasses*) Long life! Good cheer!

FALSTAFF[51]
Boys, we are off to the wars tomorrow. We'll through Gloucestershire, and there will we visit Master Robert Shallow.

HOSTESS, HAL, BARDOLPH, PISTOL, CROWD
Esquire.

Laughter, winks, and nudges among the men, who know all about Falstaff's designs on Shallow.

FALSTAFF[52]
(*Rubs the imaginary wax between his fingers.*) I have him tempering between my finger and my thumb, and shortly will I seal with him. (*Presses his thumb down as if sealing. More merriment and back slapping.*) Hal, thou must to court. Thou wilt be horribly chid tomorrow when thou com'st to thy father. Let us practice an answer.

HAL (Falstaff)[53]
What? Shall we be merry? Shall we have a play, *extempore*?

---

[51] Adapted from H IV 2, 4, 3
[52] The first sentence is adapted from H IV 2, 4, 3. Also, "Well," not "Hal" in the second sentence.
[53] Transferred from earlier in the scene.

HOSTESS, FALSTAFF, CROWD
A play, a play, *extempore*?

HAL
Do thou stand for my father, and examine me upon the particulars of my life.

HOSTESS, BARDOLPH, PISTOL, CROWD
Do it, Sir John!

FALSTAFF
(*Mulling it over*) Shall I? Content!
Raucous laughter. The Falstaffians and company leap into action, clearing the table and setting a stool on it. They move the other benches and stools away, leaving one as a step. Then they help Falstaff up, and retire to their seats. From this point forward, all save Hal and Falstaff, including Bardolph and Pistol, continue laughing when not singing.

FALSTAFF
This chair shall be my state, this dagger my sceptre, and this cushion my crown.

HOSTESS
(*Runs forward, clapping.*) O Jesu! This is excellent sport, in faith!

HOSTESS, HAL, BARDOLPH, PISTOL, CROWD
In faith, in faith!

FALSTAFF
For God's sake, lords, convey my tristful queen, for tears do stop the floodgates of her eyes.

CHORUS
God save the queen!

Hostess acts out the tristful queen as the "lords" escort her lugubriously back to her seat. Laughter continues.

FALSTAFF
There is a thing, Harry, that thou hast often heard of, …

HOSTESS, BARDOLPH, PISTOL, CROWD
Tell us what!

FALSTAFF
… and it is known to many in our land by the name of pitch.

HOSTESS, BARDOLPH, PISTOL, CROWD
Watch out, your Grace! Watch out, watch out!

FALSTAFF
This pitch, as ancient writers do report, doth defile; …

HOSTESS, BARDOLPH, PISTOL, CROWD
Scrape your boots!

FALSTAFF
… so doth the company thou keepest.

HOSTESS, BARDOLPH, PISTOL, CROWD
God's truth, Sir John! We've led his Grace astray!

FALSTAFF
(*In mock piety*) For, Harry, now I do not speak to thee in drink, but in tears, not in pleasure, but in passion, not in words only, but in woes also. And yet there is a virtuous man …

HOSTESS, BARDOLPH, PISTOL, CROWD
Now who might that be? (*Humming*) Mm.

FALSTAFF
… whom I have often noted in thy company, but I know not his name. A goodly portly man, in faith, and a corpulent; of a cheerful look, a pleasing eye, and a most noble carriage; (*With a few stately dance steps to show his noble carriage as laughter continues*) And, as I think, his age some fifty, …

HOSTESS, HAL, BARDOLPH, PISTOL, CROWD
Long since, long since, Sir John!

FALSTAFF
... or, by our Lady, inclining to three score.

HOSTESS, HAL, BARDOLPH, PISTOL, CROWD
And many more!

FALSTAFF
And now I remember me: his name is Falstaff.

HOSTESS, HAL, BARDOLPH, PISTOL, CROWD
... Falstaff (*in unison with Falstaff. Laughter resumes.*)

FALSTAFF
Him keep with; the rest banish.

PISTOL
(*Playing along*) I'm out, boys!

BARDOLPH
(*Likewise*) Me too!

HOSTESS, BARDOLPH, PISTOL, CROWD
All of us are gone!

HAL
Bravo, Jack!

HOSTESS, BARDOLPH, PISTOL, CROWD
Well done, Sir John!

HAL[54]
Now do thou stand for me, and I'll play my father!

FALSTAFF
Depose me? If thou doth it half so gravely, so majestically, hang me up by the heels for a rabbit-sucker, or a poulter's hare!

---

[54] "Now" is added.

Applauding, and cheering, the Falstaffians and company help their master down. Hal springs up in his place. Cries of: "Bravo, Sir John," *and* "your turn, your Highness!"

HAL
Swearest thou, ungracious boy? Henceforth ne'er look on me.

HOSTESS, BARDOLPH, PISTOL, CROWD
Shut your eyes, Sir John! (*Laughter continues throughout.*)

HAL
There is a devil haunts thee …

HOSTESS, BARDOLPH, PISTOL, CROWD
Fear the devil!

HAL
… in the likeness of an old fat man.

HOSTESS, BARDOLPH, PISTOL, CROWD
Guess who, Sir John?

HAL
Why dost thou converse with that trunk of humors, …

HOSTESS, BARDOLPH, PISTOL, CROWD
Guess who, Sir John, guess who!

HAL
… that bolting hutch of beastliness, that swollen parcel of dropsies, that huge bombard of sack, that roasted Manningtree ox with the pudding in his belly, that reverend vice, that grey iniquity, that father ruffian, that vanity in years? Wherein neat and cleanly, but to carve a capon and eat it? Wherein cunning, but in craft? Wherein crafty, but in villainy? Wherein villainous, but in all things? Wherein worthy, but in nothing?

FALSTAFF
I would your Grace would take me with you. Whom means your Grace?

HAL
That villainous, abominable misleader of youth, Falstaff, that old white-bearded Satan.

FALSTAFF
My lord, the man I know.

HAL
(*Aside*) I know thou dost.

This time the crowd becomes transfixed; no laughter.

FALSTAFF[55]
That he is old, the more the pity, his white hairs do witness it. No, my good lord, banish Pistol, banish Bardolph, banish Boy, banish Nell, but for sweet Jack Falstaff, kind Jack Falstaff, true Jack Falstaff, valiant Jack Falstaff; and therefore more valiant, being, as he is, old Jack Falstaff, banish not him thy Harry's company, banish Plump Jack, and banish all the world!

HAL[56]
I do, I will. (*Loud knocking at the door. Hal jumps down from the table.*) Look to the door there, lads! (*Bardolph and Pistol rush to open the door. Boy runs in, kneels to Hal.*) Boy, what news?

BOY (Peto)[57]
(*Rising*) The king your father is at Westminster, and there are twenty weak and weary posts come from the north, and as I came along, I met and overtook a dozen captains, bareheaded, sweating, knocking at the taverns, (*Daggers drawn, Pistol and Bardolph scramble to guard the door.*) mustering levies, haling up deserters, and asking every one for Sir John Falstaff.

---

[55] Originally "banish Peto, banish Bardolph, banish Poins, ..."
[56] "Peto, how now, what news?" This and the following lines are taken from H IV 2, 2, 4.
[57] "mustering ... deserters" is added.

HAL[58]
By heaven, Boy, I feel me much to blame so idly to profane the precious time. Give me my sword and cloak. (*Boy rushes to get them.*) Falstaff, good night. (*Exit Hal.*)

Loud knocking again..

FALSTAFF
More knocking? What now, Bardolph?

Bardolph exits and returns almost immediately.

BARDOLPH
You must away to court, sir, presently. A dozen captains stay at door for you.

FIRST CAPTAIN
(*Offstage*) Sir John Falstaff!

SECOND CAPTAIN
(*Offstage*) We'll bear no shirkers and malingerers!

FALSTAFF[59]
(*Speaking to Hostess*) You see, my good wench, how men of merit are sought after. The undeserver may sleep when the man of action is called on. (*Sings.*) To arms, lads. Tell them I come. (*Pistol and Bardolph each take a helmet, cuirass and sword from a cupboard upstage, then exeunt with Boy and all others except Falstaff and Hostess.*) Now comes in the sweetest morsel of the night, and we must hence, and leave it unpicked.

HOSTESS (Doll Tearsheet)
Well, sweet Jack, have a care of thyself. Ah, rogue, in faith I love thee. By my troth, I kiss thee with a most constant heart. (*Kisses him.*)

---

[58] "Poins," not "Boy"
[59] "wenches," not "wench"

FALSTAFF[60]
Ah, Nell, thou dost give me but flattering kisses. Thou'lt forget me when I am gone.

HOSTESS (Doll Tearsheet)[61]
By the mass, thou'lt set me a-weeping if thou say'st so. (*She weeps silently.*) Prove that I ever dress myself handsome till thy return.

FALSTAFF[62]
I am old, Nell, I am old.

HOSTESS (Doll Tearsheet)[63]
I love thee better than I love e'er a scurvy young boy of them all. But when wilt thou leave fighting o' days and drinking o' nights, and begin to patch up thine old body for heaven?

FALSTAFF[64]
Peace, good Nell, do not speak like a death's head. Do not bid me remember mine end.

HOSTESS
Well, fare thee well. I have known thee these twenty-nine years, come peascod time, but an honester and truer-hearted man ...

She weeps. Falstaff takes her in his arms. Pounding on the door.

FIRST CAPTAIN, SECOND CAPTAIN
(*Offstage*) Sir John, Sir John!

FALSTAFF
Will you brawl? Will you riot at an honest widow's hostel? Let Scots and Welsh beware: Jack Falstaff comes! (*Spoken softly and in earnest*) Sweet Nell, wish me Godspeed. (*Singing*) London, farewell, and welcome, Gloucestershire!

---

[60] "Ah, Nell" is added. "Busses," not "kisses."
[61] "By my troth," not "By the mass."
[62] "Nell" is added.
[63] "foining," not "fighting"
[64] "Doll," not "Nell"

Falstaff puts on his cuirass, hoists his sword belt over his shoulder, puts on his helmet, and strides to the door. At his most imperious, he throws wide the door and stares down the captains. He then turns to Hostess, with a deep and courtly bow. Exit Falstaff. Blackout.

ACT II

Act 2, Scene 1 *"Shallow's Orchard"* (From H IV 2, 3, 2)

We are in Shallow's Orchard, bordering a forest. Enter Falstaff, Bardolph, Boy and Shallow. The first three are in armor. Shallow dodders along with a walking stick, showing them around.

FALSTAFF
I am glad to see you, by my troth, Master Shallow.

SHALLOW
(*In an old man's reedy treble*) O, Sir John, do you remember since we lay all night in the windmill in Saint George's Field?[65]

FALSTAFF
No more of that, good Master Shallow, no more of that.

SHALLOW
Ha! 'twas a merry night! And is Jane Nightwork alive?

FALSTAFF
She lives, Master Shallow.

SHALLOW
(*Ruefully*) She never would away with me.

FALSTAFF
Never, never, she would always say she could not abide Master Shallow.

---

[65] A well-known London bawdy-house in Shakespeare's day

SHALLOW

(*Rueful again*) By the Mass, I could anger her to the heart. (*Lurches forward as if to grab Jane's ample flesh*) She was then a bona-roba![66] (*Suddenly apprehensive*) Doth she hold her own well?

FALSTAFF

Old, old, Master Shallow.

SHALLOW

Nay, she must be old, she cannot choose but be old, certain she's old, and had Robin Nightwork by Old Nightwork before I came to Clement's Inn.[67]

FALSTAFF[68]

That's fifty-five years ago.

SHALLOW[69]

(*To Boy*) Ha, little soldier, that thou had'st seen that that this knight and I have seen! Ha, Sir John, said I well?

FALSTAFF

We have heard the chimes at midnight, Master Shallow.

SHALLOW

That we have, that we have, that we have, in faith, Sir John, we have. Our watchword was (*He strikes a drinking pose.*) "Hem, boys!"[70] Come, let's to dinner, come, let's to dinner. Jesus! The days that we have seen! Come, come!

Exeunt all but Falstaff. Falstaff waves after them.

FALSTAFF

Fare you well, gentle gentlemen. As I return, I will fetch off[71] this justice. I do see the bottom of Justice Shallow. Lord, Lord, (*Sanctimoniously*) how subject

---

[66] Hot stuff
[67] A law school in London
[68] "year," not "years"
[69] "cousin Silence," not "little soldier"
[70] Down the hatch!
[71] Swindle

we old men are to this vice of lying. This same starved justice hath done nothing but prate to me of the wildness of his youth, and the feats he hath done about Turnbull Street, and every third word a lie. I do remember him at Clement's Inn, like a man made after supper of a cheese-paring. When he was naked, he was for all the world like a forked radish with a head fantastically carved upon it with a knife. He came ever in the rearward of the fashion, and sang (*Sweetly*) those tunes to the over-scutched hussies (*Sarcastically again*) that he heard the carman whistle,[72] and swore they were his fancies or his good-nights. And now is this Vice's dagger become a squire, and now has he lands and beefs. Well, I'll be acquainted with him as I return, and it shall go hard, but I'll make him a philosopher's two stones[73] to me. (*Lightly, jauntily*) If the young dace[74] be a bait for the old pike, I see no reason (*Piously, in the nasal drone of the cleric*) in the law of nature, (*Back in character*) but I may snap at him. Let time shape, and there an end.

Exit Falstaff.

Act 2, Scene 2 *"Jerusalem"* (From H IV 2, 4, 4 and H IV 2, 4, 5)

The Presence Chamber in Westminster with Henry IV, Chief Justice, Clarence and attendants. The first two are studying documents in silence. Clarence is kneeling at a prie-dieu.

CLARENCE AND OFFSTAGE CHORUS
Veni, Sancte Spiritus, Veni, Redemptor Mundi.
Kyrie eleison, Christe eleison, Kyrie eleison.

Enter Warwick.

HENRY IV
Who's there? The Duke of Warwick?[75]

---

[72] The two main tunes of "The Carman's Whistle" are quoted here.
[73] Sources of wealth
[74] Kind of fish
[75] Pronounced "Warrick"

WARWICK (Westmoreland)
Health to my sovereign, and new happiness
Added to that that I am to deliver!
Mowbray, the Bishop Scroop, Hastings and all
Are brought to the correction of your law.
There is not now a rebel's sword unsheathed,
But Peace puts out her olive everywhere.

HENRY IV[76]
O Warwick, Warwick, thou'rt a summer bird
Which ever in the haunch of winter sings
The lifting up of day.

Peals of church bells are heard.

CLARENCE (Harcourt)
Look, here's more news!

Enter a messenger. He hands the Chief Justice a packet, then exits as Chief Justice scans the contents. At the King's gesture, a servant closes the window.

CHIEF JUSTICE (Harcourt)
From enemies heaven keep your majesty,
And when they stand against you, may they fall,
As those this packet tells[77] you of. The Earl
Northumberland, and the Lord Fawconbridge,
With a great power of English and of Scots,
Are by your son Prince Harry[78] overthrown.
To tell you how this action hath been borne,
He will himself arrive within the night.
All rejoice. The King suddenly collapses. All rush to him.

---

[76] "Westmoreland," not "Warwick"
[77] "that I am come to tell," not "As those this packet tells"
[78] "the Shrieve of Yorkshire," not "your son Prince Harry"

HENRY IV
And wherefore should these good news make me sick?
I should rejoice now at this happy news,
And now my sight fails, and my brain is giddy.
O me! Come near me! Now I am much ill.

OFFSTAGE CHORUS
Veni, Sancte Spiritus, Veni, Redemptor Mundi, Veni, Sancte Spiritus.

CLARENCE (Gloucester)
Comfort, your majesty!

CHIEF JUSTICE (Warwick)
Be patient, Prince, for you do know these fits
Are with his Highness very ordinary.
Stand from him. Give him air. He'll straight be well.

OFFSTAGE CHORUS
Kyrie eleison, Christe eleison, Kyrie eleison.

CLARENCE[79]
No, no, he cannot long hold out these pangs.
The river hath thrice flowed, no ebb between,
Just as the old folk tell us that it did
When our great grandsire, Edward, sicked and died.

CHIEF JUSTICE (Warwick)[80]
Speak lower, Prince, for now the king recovers.

HENRY IV
I pray you, take me up, and bear me hence
Into some other chamber. Softly, pray.

WARWICK
(*To Clarence and Chief Justice*) Lords, with your leave, I must inform the Council.

---

[79] The last two lines condense and approximate.
[80] "Princes," not "Prince"

Upon a Day | 111

Exit Warwick. The stage darkens except in the area of Henry IV and those near him. The retainers come forward; all bear him to an adjoining room. The light tracks, so that the throne is no longer visible.

CLARENCE
His eye is hollow, and he changes much.

They lay him on a couch.

CHIEF JUSTICE (Warwick)
Less noise, less noise.

Another spotlight finds Hal, in a jaunty mood, entering the Presence Chamber from which his father has just been carried.

HAL
Who saw the Duke of Clarence?

CLARENCE
(*Crossing to Hal*) I am here, brother, full of heaviness.
Hal puts his arm around his younger brother to jolly him up.

HAL
How now! Rain within doors, and none abroad?
How doth the king?

CLARENCE
(*Clarence turns so that Hal can see his tears.*) Exceedingly ill.

This hits Hal like a shot. Clarence leads him to the King and Chief Justice. The second spotlight tracks, and merges with the first.

HAL
(*As they move*) Heard he the good news yet?
Tell it him!

CHIEF JUSTICE (Warwick)
Not so much noise, my lords. Sweet Prince, speak low.
The king your father is disposed to sleep.

CLARENCE (Warwick)
(*To Hal*) Will't please your grace to go along with us?

HAL
No, I will sit and watch here by the king.

Exeunt all but Hal and Henry IV. Hal sits at the bedside.

HENRY IV
(*Waking*) Come hither, Harry, sit thou by my bed,
And hear, I think, the very latest counsel
That ever I shall breathe. (*Hal kneels.*) God knows, my son,
By what bypaths and indirect crooked ways
I met the crown, and I myself know well
How troublesome it sat upon my head.
To thee it shall descend with better quiet,
Better opinion, better confirmation,
For all the soil of its achievement goes
With me into the earth.
More would I, but my lungs are wasted so
That strength of speech is utterly denied me.
How I came by the crown, O God forgive,
And grant it may with thee in true peace live.

Father and son embrace. Enter Clarence.

Look, look, here comes my Thomas. Welcome, son![81]

CLARENCE (Prince John)
Health, peace and happiness to my royal father!

HENRY IV
Thou brings't me happiness and peace, son Thomas.[82]
But health, alack, with youthful wings is flown
From this bare withered trunk. Upon thy sight
My worldly business makes a period.

---

[81] "my John of Lancaster," not "Thomas. Welcome, son!"
[82] "son John," not "son Thomas"

Where is my Lord Chief Justice?[83]

HAL
(*Calling*) My Lord Chief Justice![84]

Enter Chief Justice.

CLARENCE, OFFSTAGE CHORUS
(*Continuing as Henry IV and Chief Justice sing.*) In manus tuas, Domine, commendo spiritum meum. Sicut erat in principio, et nunc, et semper, et in secula seculorum. Salva nos, Domine, vigilantes, custodi nos dormientes. Nunc dimittis servum tuum Domine, secundum verbum tuum in pace; Quia viderunt oculi mei salutare tuum; Requiescat in pace.

HENRY IV[85]
Doth any name particular belong unto this lodging?

The circle of light widens to reveal a simple bedchamber.

CHIEF JUSTICE (Warwick)
'Tis called Jerusalem, my noble lord.

Slowly, the walls of the bedchamber dissolve to reveal the hill of Jerusalem under the stars.

HENRY IV[86]
Praise be to God! Even here my life must end.
It hath been prophesied to me many years,
I should not die but in Jerusalem,
Which vainly I supposed the Holy Land.
God led us to this chamber; here I'll lie.
In this Jerusalem shall Harry die.

---

[83] "Lord of Warwick," not "Lord Chief Justice"
[84] Ibid.
[85] "Unto the lodging where I first did swoon?"
[86] "Laud," not "Praise"

The King dies. The Chief Justice kneels before Hal, removes a chain with a large medallion from his shoulders and presents it. Hal puts it back over the old man's shoulders and helps him to his feet.

Act 2, Scene 3 *"Davy's Ledger"* (From H IV 2, 5, 1)

We are in Shallow's house. It is daylight outside. We see a table upstage, and a chair and reading desk downstage. Shallow, in a merry mood, is looking for something. Drawers and cupboards have been opened and articles dumped on the floor.

SHALLOW
(*Calling into a wing*) Davy! Where in the world is the silver?

DAVY
(*Offstage*) In a moment, sir.

Shallow resumes his search, whistling and humming.

SHALLOW
Davy! Where's the service? Food must be served for our guests.

DAVY
(*Offstage*) In a moment, sir.

SHALLOW[87]
(*Calling in the opposite direction*) By cock and pie, Sir John, you shall not away without dinner tonight!

FALSTAFF[88]
(*Offstage*) Pray you excuse me, Master Robert Shallow. I must a dozen mile tonight.

---

[87] "without dinner" is added.
[88] The last sentence is taken from H IV 2, 3, 2.

SHALLOW
I will not excuse you, you will not be excused, excuses shall not be admitted, there is no excuse shall serve, you shall not be excused! (*Shallow muscles a chest in front of a high cupboard, perhaps balancing a chair or stool or both on it, and pauses to judge distances to the closed top doors.*) What, Davy, I say! Nothing is where I can find it.

DAVY
(*Still offstage*) In a moment, sir.

SHALLOW[89]
(*Shallow begins his climb.*) Sir John, you must dine! You will not be excused!

Shallow reaches the doors and tugs them. They stick. He yanks harder. As the doors fly open, Shallow loses his balance. Pillows, feathers and papers tumble out. Shallow's fall is as comical and convoluted as resources and tumbling skills allow. Enter Davy with from four to eight servants plus a clerk with a ledger. All are deadpan and super-efficient. Davy claps his hands. Two servants gently deposit Shallow in a chair, then carry it and him to the desk. Meanwhile, others open the chest and start laying the table from it. The clerk puts the ledger on the desk before Shallow. Davy opens it and points.

DAVY
(*Speaking*) Your worship, if I may draw your attention to these entries. Marry, sir, such extravagance **cannot** be borne.

SHALLOW
(*Studying the ledger*) Davy, Davy, (*Turns a page.*) let me see, Davy. (*We see that Shallow is unfazed by his fall and Davy's snit, and is as merry as ever.*)

DAVY[90]
(*Davy turns another page and taps the ledger for emphasis.*) And **again**, sir, **shall** we sow the headland with wheat?

---

[89] "you must dine!" is added.
[90] "hade land," not "headland"

SHALLOW[91]
With red wheat, Davy. And William cook, bid him come hither. Sir John!

Davy gestures, and a servant runs off for the cook.

DAVY[92]
And **when**, sir, shall we settle the smith's note for shoeing and plow-irons?

SHALLOW[93]
Let it be cast and paid. (*Davy points and the clerk writes.*) Sir John, you shall not be excused! (*The cook runs in.*) Ah, William, some pigeons tonight, William, and a couple of short-legged hens, a joint of mutton, and any pretty tiny little kickshaws. (*Conducts an imaginary orchestra to the tune.*) And ready the broth at once. (*The cook bustles off.*) Where are you, Sir John?

At Davy's gesture, a handyman runs in and holds up a bucket by its broken chain.

DAVY[94]
And now, sir, a new link to the bucket **must** be had.

SHALLOW[95]
Look to it, Davy. Sir John, you must dine. (*Again Davy gestures. The handyman runs off with the bucket. The clerk writes, then exits with the ledger. Enter Falstaff, Bardolph and Boy. The men are still in their cuirasses. Shallow rises to greet them.*) Come, Sir John, come all, come to dinner. Spread, Davy, spread. (*Davy and the servants begin putting food on the table.*) Come, Master Bardolph, and (*Patting Boy on the head*) welcome to you, my tall fellow. Off with your boots, Sir John!

DAVY
(*Indicating Falstaff*) Doth the man of war stay all night, sir?

---

[91] "But for," not "and"
[92] "Here is now," not "And when, sir, shall we settle"
[93] All to Davy, not William. William does not appear.
[94] "And" is added.
[95] "Come … dinner" is added. "Spread, Davy, spread" is taken from H IV 2, 5, 3.

SHALLOW

Yea, Davy. I will use him well. (*Shallow taps his foot to the tune, with a finger alongside his nose and a wink toward Falstaff.*) A friend in the court is better than a penny in purse. (*Falstaff is meant to hear this, and does. He taps his lips for mock secrecy. Bardolph lifts a thumb-to-forefinger "It's in the bag" gesture. Shallow indicates Bardolph.*) Use his men well, Davy, for they are arrant knaves, and will backbite.

DAVY

No worse than they are backbitten, sir, for they have marvelous foul linen.

SHALLOW

(*Applauding*) Well conceited, Davy. About thy business, Davy.

DAVY[96]

First, sir, I beseech you to countenance William Visor of Woncot against Clement Perkes of the Inn.

SHALLOW

There are many complaints, Davy, against that Visor. That Visor is an arrant knave, upon my knowledge.

DAVY

I grant your worship that he is a knave, sir, but a knave should have some countenance at a friend's request. An honest man, sir, is able to speak for himself, when a knave is not. If I cannot once or twice in a quarter bear out a knave against an honest man, I have but very little credit with your worship. The knave is mine honest friend, sir. Therefore, beseech you, let him be countenanced. (*Stamps his foot.*)

SHALLOW

(*Amused*) Go to, I say he shall have no wrong. Look about, Davy. (*Exit Davy.*) Come, Sir John, come to dinner. You shall not be excused.

---

[96] "I beseech you, sir," not "First, sir, I beseech you"

FALSTAFF[97]
I'll follow you, good Master Shallow. (*Shallow, Bardolph and Boy go to the table and sit. The broth and wine arrive and are served. Falstaff remains in the chair.*) If I were sawed into quantities, I would make four dozen of such bearded hermit staves as Master Shallow. I will devise enough matter out of him to keep Prince Harry in continual laughter the wearing out of six fashions. O, I will make him laugh 'til his face be like a wet cloak ill laid up!

SHALLOW
Sir John!

FALSTAFF
(*Suppressing laughter*) I come, Master Shallow, I come, Master Shallow.

Falstaff rises and walks toward the table. All raise their glasses to him. He pauses, arms outspread to acknowledge their greeting. Unseen by them, Davy takes a nip from the wine flask.

Act 2, Scene 4 *"Pistol's News"* (From H IV 2, 5, 3)

Lights up on Shallow's house as before. It is night. Falstaff, Shallow, Bardolph and Boy are at table. The men have all drunk heavily. Boy is asleep in his chair. Musicians play. Davy and a plentitude of well-liveried servants keep the men's glasses filled with wine. Davy and the servants and musicians help themselves to some whenever the rest are not looking. Davy is thoroughly plastered, and untypically benign.

SHALLOW, FALSTAFF, BARDOLPH, PISTOL, DAVY AND SERVANTS
Tapster, drinker, fill another ale anon!

FALSTAFF[98]
'Fore God, Master Shallow, you have here a goodly dwelling and a rich.

---

[97] Condensed. "matter enough out of this Shallow," not "enough matter out of him." "You shall see," not "I will make"
[98] "Master Shallow" is added.

Falstaff makes a "you-know-what-I-mean" sign to Bardolph. Laughter. Boy wakes up.

BARDOLPH
God's truth, Sir John!

BOY
(*To Shallow*) Health to your worship!

SHALLOW[99]
Barren, barren, barren. Beggars all, beggars all, Sir John. By the Mass, I have drunk too much already!

FALSTAFF
No, no!

BARDOLPH
Not a bit!

BOY
Good Cheer!

SHALLOW
Give Master Bardolph some wine, Davy!

BOY
A song, your worship!

BARDOLPH
That's the spirit!

FALSTAFF
Let's have a song, Master Shallow!

Davy pours for all, and sneaks some more himself. Shallow rises to sing and gestures to musicians, who move forward. Boy drifts off again.

---

[99] "at supper," not "already"

DAVY (Silence) [100]
(*Preempting Shallow as he is about to begin*) Do nothing but drink, and make good cheer, And praise God for the merry year,

SHALLOW, FALSTAFF, BARDOLPH, SERVANTS
(*In unison with Davy*) Praise God for the merry year,

FALSTAFF
Go to it, Davy!

BARDOLPH
Hurrah, Davy!

DAVY, SHALLOW AND SERVANTS (Silence)
When flesh is cheap, and females dear,

Falstaff does a double take.

DAVY (Silence)
And lusty lads roam here and there
So merrily,

Boy wakes up.

ALL THE MEN AND BOY (Silence alone)
And ever among so merrily.

Laughter and roars of approval. The musicians retire to the background. Boy drifts off again.

FALSTAFF
There's a merry heart!

BARDOLPH (Falstaff)[101]
Good Master Davy, I'll give you a health for that anon.

---

[100] "eat," not "drink"
[101] "Silence," not "Davy"

SHALLOW[102]
Health, Sir John! What you want in meat, we'll have in drink; (*Murmurs of appreciation from Falstaff and Bardolph.*) the heart's all. Be merry, masters, and (*To Boy, who is still asleep*) merry dreams, my little soldier there. Pour, Davy, pour.

Davy does so, and conducts the musicians with his other hand. Falstaff rises to toast Shallow. Again, Davy jumps in first.

DAVY (Silence)
Be merry, be merry, my wife has all,
For women are shrews, both short and tall.

Boy awakes again.

ALL (Silence)
'Tis merry in hall, when beards wag all,
And welcome merry Shrove-tide.
Be merry, be merry.

Shouts of approval. Again the musicians retire, and Boy drifts off.

FALSTAFF[103]
(*Aside to Shallow*) I did not think Master Davy had been a man of this mettle.

DAVY (Silence)
Who, I? I have been merry twice and once ere now. (*With a few dance steps*)

BARDOLPH[104]
(*Rising*) Health and long life to you, Master Davy.

SHALLOW
(*Rising*) Health to you, Master Bardolph. (*To Boy, still asleep*) Health to my little tiny thief, and to all the cabileros about London.

---

[102] The second line is Davy's. The others are loosely adapted from Shallow's.
[103] "Silence," not "Davy"
[104] Ibid.

Again, Falstaff rises and the musicians come forward. Boy wakes up again. Davy pours wine, and nips some. Falstaff, Shallow and Bardolph are about to join in a toast. But by now they have learned that Davy is sure to come first, so they defer graciously.

DAVY, FALSTAFF, SHALLOW, BARDOLPH AND SERVANTS (Silence alone)
(*Davy fills the men's glasses and leads, followed by the others*) Fill the cup, and let it come. I'll pledge you a mile …

DAVY (Silence)
… to the bottom.

They hold out their glasses bottoms up. Meanwhile Davy, behind them, drains the pitcher. Boy drifts off again. Davy collapses, dead drunk. So then do Shallow and all servants and musicians. Another servant rushes in, props Shallow in a chair, speaks inaudibly to Bardolph, and exits.

BARDOLPH (Davy) [105]
(*To Falstaff*) Your worship, here's Pistol come from the court with news.

FALSTAFF
From the court? Let him come in. (*Bardolph opens the door, then also collapses as Pistol enters.*) How now, Pistol!

PISTOL
Sweet knight, thou art now one of the greatest men in this realm. (*Pistol rushes to Falstaff and kneels. Knowing Pistol, Falstaff takes this tongue-in-cheek.*) Sir John, I am thy Pistol and thy friend, and helter-skelter have I rode to thee, and tidings do I bring, and lucky joys, and golden times and happy news of price.

Bardolph and Boy have awoken during this. They laugh and applaud.

FALSTAFF
(*Drily, with a wink to Bardolph*) I pray thee now, deliver them like a man of **this** world.

---

[105] Loosely adapted

Bardolph and Boy laugh again.

PISTOL
A foutre[106] for the world and worldlings base! (*Laughter.*)
I speak of Africa and golden joys.

BARDOLPH, BOY
Bravo, Pistol!

FALSTAFF
(*In the same fustian vein, with sweeping gestures and rolling eyes*) O base Assyrian knight, what is thy news? Let King Cophetua know the truth thereof.

Bardolph and Boy crack up. Pistol glares at them.

PISTOL
Shall dunghill curs confront the Helicons?
And shall good news be baffled?
Then, Pistol, lay thy head in Furies' lap.

The picture of wounded dignity, Pistol lays his head to the floor. Falstaff, unable to pry the news out of him, throws up his hands in good-natured surrender. Bardolph and Boy are convulsed. All this is enough to bring Shallow half-awake.

SHALLOW
(*To Pistol, drowsily*) Honest gentleman, I know not your breeding. I am, Sir, under the king, (*Yawns or belches.*) in some authority.

PISTOL
(*Rising*) Under which king, Besonian? Speak, or die! (*Puts hand to sword hilt.*)

SHALLOW
(*Amused, plays along as if in a knock-knock joke.*) Under King Harry.

PISTOL
Harry the Fourth, or Fifth?

---

[106] Fig. Pistol raises his thumbs between his fingers.

Falstaff, Boy and Bardolph pop their eyes open. All hold their breaths. Shallow, last to catch on, is still playing the knock-knock joke.

SHALLOW
Harry the Fourth.

PISTOL
(*As before*) A foutre for thine office! Sir John, thy tender lambkin now is king!

Falstaff, Boy and Bardolph rise, thunderstruck.

FALSTAFF
(*Rising*) What! Is the old king dead?

PISTOL
As nail in door. The things I speak are just.

Shallow, Bardolph and Boy jump to their feet.

FALSTAFF
Away, Bardolph! Saddle my horse. (*Exit Bardolph.*) Master Robert Shallow, choose what office thou wilt in the land, 'tis thine. Master Shallow, Lord Shallow, be as thou wilt; I am fortune's steward. Get on thy boots, we'll ride all night. Boy, to horse! (*Exit Boy.*) I know the young king is sick for me. Let us take any man's horses: the laws of England are at my commandment. Blessed are they that have been my friends, and woe to my Lord Chief Justice!

Pistol, with a toothy grin, draws a forefinger slowly across his throat. Lights out.

Act 2, Scene 5 *"Banishment"* (From H IV 2, 5, 5)

Westminster, near the Abbey. A threatening storm.

MONKS
(*Offstage, from the Abbey*) Judica me, Deus, et discerne causam meam de gente non sancta. Ab homine iniquo et doloso eripe me. A viro iniquo eripies me.

Crowd noise begins to be heard offstage. Enter Hostess, Boy and Bardolph spreading rushes.

HOSTESS (First Groom)[107]
More rushes, more rushes!

BOY (Second Groom)
The trumpets have sounded twice.

Lightning (near) as offstage crowd noise continues.

BARDOLPH (Third Groom)
'Twill be two o'clock ere they come from the coronation.

BOY
Dispatch, dispatch.

The offstage crowd noise grows. The crowd starts pouring in. Falstaff, Pistol and Shallow are among them. The crowd, having been talking aloud, now mimes conversation.

FALSTAFF
Stand here by me, Master Robert Shallow. I will make the King do you grace: I will leer upon him as he comes by, and do but mark the countenance (*Mugging*) that he will give me.

PISTOL
God bless thy lungs, good knight.

FALSTAFF[108]
Come here, Pistol, stand behind me. O, Master Shallow, if I had had time to have made new liveries, I would have bestowed the thousand pound I borrowed of you. (*Innocently, but with a broad wink visible only to Pistol and Bardolph. They break up.*) But 'tis no matter, this poor show doth better, this doth infer the zeal I had to see him.

---

[107] Hostess is not in this scene in the play.
[108] "Master shallow" is added.

SHALLOW
It doth so.

FALSTAFF
It shows my earnestness of affection, …

SHALLOW
It doth so.

FALSTAFF
… my devotion, …

SHALLOW
It doth, it doth, it doth.

FALSTAFF
… as it were, to ride day and night, and not to deliberate, not to remember, not to have patience to shift me, …

SHALLOW
It is best, certain.

Lightning, near.

FALSTAFF
… but to stand stained with travel and sweating with desire to see him, thinking of nothing else, (*Lightning, near.*) putting all affairs else in oblivion, (*Lightning, near. It begins to snow.*) as if there were nothing else to be done but to see him.

Shouts offstage. The crowd stops miming conversation and listens. Another crowd roar offstage.

HOSTESS
(*Shouting*) The king! The king!

BARDOLPH, CROWD
(*Shouting*) God save the king!

Everyone rushes to get a better view.

BARDOLPH
I see them!

The crowd roars.

PISTOL
There roared the sea, and trumpet-clangor sounds!

A piper emerges from the crowd and plays. Hostess sings with him. The crowd grows silent.

HOSTESS[109]
(Simply, with quiet faith) Enforce we us with all our might
To love Saint George, Our Lady's knight.

BOY, HOSTESS
In his virtue he will us lead;
The foe him see foremost in fight.

BOY, HOSTESS, SHALLOW, FALSTAFF, BARDOLPH, PISTOL
To worship George then have we need,
Which is our sov'reign Lady's knight.

ALL WITH THE CROWD
Enforce we us with all our might
To love Saint George, Our Lady's knight.
In his virtue he will us lead;
The foe him see foremost in fight.
To worship George then have we need,
Which is our sov'reign Lady's knight.

The crowd cheers and roars as the King's train begins to enter.

BARDOLPH
(*Shouting*) God for Saint George!

---

[109] The words and music quote the Second Agincourt Song.

The crowd roars again.

FALSTAFF
God save thy Grace, King Hal, my royal Hal!

The crowd roars again.

BOY
(*Shouting*) King Harry!

Others shout the same.

PISTOL
The heav'ns thee guard and keep, most royal imp of fame!

The crowd roars again.

FALSTAFF
God save thee, my sweet boy! (*Enter Clarence, Warwick and Hartcourt. Crowd roar is at maximum.*) My king, my Jove! (*Enter Chief Justice, followed by roars from the crowd. Enter the King. All but Falstaff drop to their knees, silent. Falstaff runs into the road, brushing past the Chief Justice. He falls on his knees before the King, his arms outstretched in greeting.*) I speak to thee, ... (*With a gesture, the King stops the procession. Falstaff falters.*) ... my heart.

A long and painful silence as the King stares him down. Falstaff collapses to all fours in the road.

HENRY V (Formerly HAL)
(*With icy scorn*) I know thee not, old man. Fall to thy prayers.
How ill white hairs become a fool and jester!
Leave gormandizing. Know that the grave doth gape
For thee thrice wider than for other men.
Reply not to me with a fool-born jest.
Presume not that I am the thing I was,
For God doth know, so shall the world perceive,
That I have turned away my former self:
So will I those that kept me company.
When thou dost hear I am as I have been,

Approach me, and thou shalt be as thou wast:
The tutor and the feeder of my riots.
Till then I banish thee, on pain of death,
As I have done the rest of my misleaders,
Not to come near our person by ten mile.
Set on.

Falstaff falls prone. The procession resumes. Crowd roars offstage, ahead of it. Exeunt the King and his train. The crowd follows. Falstaff remains prone, dazed. Pistol, Bardolph, Boy and Shallow rise.

FALSTAFF
Master Shallow, (*He begins to rise unsteadily.*) I owe you a thousand pound.

SHALLOW
Yea, marry, Sir John, which I beseech you to let me have home with me.

FALSTAFF[110]
(*Back in character*) That can hardly be, Master Shallow. Do not you grieve at this; I shall be sent for in private to him. I shall be sent for soon at night!

Exeunt omnes. Gradually we become aware of crowd noise, faint in the distance, from the direction the King has taken.

FEMALE VOICE
God bless your majesty!

CHORUS OF MONKS
(*Offstage, from the Abbey*) Agnus Dei qui tollis peccata mundi, miserere nobis. Dona nobis pacem. Amen.

---

[110] Condensed

Act 2, Scene 6 *"Muse of Fire"* (From H V Prologue; H V 1, 2 and H V 2, 1)

Spotlight on Pistol. Stage otherwise dark.

PISTOL (Chorus)
O for a muse of fire, that would ascend
The brightest heaven of invention,
A kingdom for a stage, princes to act,
And monarchs to behold the swelling scene!
Then should the warlike Harry, like himself,
Assume the stance of Mars, and at his heels,
Leash'd in, like hounds, should famine, sword and fire
Crouch for employment.

Blackout; chorus is unseen in the darkness.

CHORUS
Now all the youth of England are on fire,
And silken dalliance in the wardrobe lies.
Now thrive the armorers, and honor's thought
Reigns solely in the breast of every man.
They sell the pasture now to buy the horse.
For now sits Expectation in the air,
And hides a sword, from hilts unto the point,
With crowns imperial, crowns and coronets,
Promised to Harry and his followers.

The crowd roars. A spotlight finds Boy, Hostess, Bardolph, Pistol, Shallow and Davy. Hostess and Pistol are arm in arm.

CHORUS (Bardolph)[111]
- Here comes ancient Pistol and his wife, for 'tis certain he is married to Nell
- Quickly.

---

[111] Adapted

BOY
Mine host Pistol, you must come to my master, and you Hostess. He's very sick and would to bed.

HOSTESS, SHALLOW, BARDOLPH, PISTOL, DAVY (Hostess alone)[112]
He'll make the crow a pudding one of these days. The king hath killed his heart.

Darkness again. Cannon in the distance. A hubbub of male voices, representing parliament. A spotlight finds the King. The others remain unseen.

HENRY V (Hal)[113]
My lords, omit no happy hour
That may give furtherance to our expedition,
For now we have no thought in us but France.

The lords roar assent.

Therefore let our proportions for these wars
Be soon collected, and all things thought upon
That may with reasonable swiftness add
More feathers to our wings; for, God before,
We'll chide this Dauphin at his father's door.

MEN OF PARLIAMENT
We'll chide this Dauphin at his father's door.

More roars of assent from the lords. Spotlight out on King. New spotlight finds Boy, Shallow, Bardolph, Pistol and Davy conversing outside Boar's Head Inn. Hostess leans out from a window.

HOSTESS[114]
As ever you came of women, come in quickly to Sir John. Ah, poor heart, he is so shaked of a burning that it is most lamentable to behold. Ah, sweet men, come to him.

All rush in. Blackout.

---

[112] "yield," not "make"
[113] From H V 1, 2
[114] From H V 2, 1

Act 2, Scene 7 *"Off to War"* (From H V 2, 3)

It is just before dawn. Pistol and Hostess stand outside Boar's Head Inn. Pistol, carrying a lantern, knocks on the door.

PISTOL[115]
Bardolph, be blithe, Boy, bristle thy courage up, (*Bardolph, Boy, Shallow and Davy emerge from the Inn, still half asleep. Boy yawns and rubs his eyes. Bardolph carries a second lantern.*) for Falstaff, (*Bardolph and Boy are suddenly wide awake and apprehensive.*) he is dead, (*Boy, Shallow, Bardolph and Davy kneel and cross themselves.*) and we must yearn therefore.

BOY, SHALLOW, BARDOLPH, PISTOL, DAVY (Bardolph alone)
(*Boy, Shallow, Bardolph and Davy remain kneeling.*) Would I were with him, wheresome'er he is, either in heaven or in hell.

Spotlight on Hostess. Boy, Shallow, Bardolph and Davy remain kneeling.

HOSTESS
Nay, sure, he's not in hell, he's in Arthur's bosom, if ever man went to Arthur's bosom. He made a finer end, and went away, an it had been any Christom child. He parted even just between twelve and one, even at the turning of the tide. For after I saw him fumble with the sheets, and play with flowers, and smile upon his fingers' ends, I knew there was but one way, for his nose was as sharp as a pen, and he babbled of green fields. 'How now, Sir John,' quoth I. 'What, man! Be of good cheer!' So he cried out, 'God, God, God,' three or four times. Now I, to comfort him, bid him he should not think of God; I hoped there was no need to trouble himself with any such thoughts yet. So he bade me lay more clothes on his feet. I put my hand into the bed, and felt them, and they were as cold as any stone. Then I felt to his knees, and so upward and upward, and all was as cold as any stone.

The sky has brightened by imperceptible degrees, and it is now first dawn. Boy, Shallow, Bardolph and Davy rise. We see that we are in the square outside Boar's Head Inn. Bardolph snuffs out the lanterns, takes them inside the inn, and returns. The square begins to fill with soldiers and common folk. Officers begin to appear along with wagonloads of armaments and military paraphernalia.

---

[115] "earn," not "yearn"

Soldiers join their units and receive pay and equipment. As sleepiness wears off, the mood becomes buoyant and patriotic. We sense that all England thrills to the martial spirit.

BARDOLPH (Nym)
Shall we shog? The king will be gone from Southampton.

SHALLOW
(As crowd noise intensifies) Londoners, up!

DAVY
Londoners, up!

BOY, SHALLOW, BARDOLPH, PISTOL, DAVY, SOLDIERS AND TOWNSFOLK
Alive, alive, alive! Eastcheap in the van!

Enter a procession headed by officers and prelates, on their way to Southampton. All others kneel and cross themselves. Priests give them absolution.

BOY, HOSTESS, SHALLOW, BARDOLPH, PISTOL, DAVY, SOLDIERS AND TOWNSFOLK
Our king sails forth to Normandy.

SHALLOW, BARDOLPH, PISTOL, DAVY, SOLDIERS
To France, to France, to France!

TOWNSWOMEN
Man of arms, go bravely, bravely forth!

As the procession exits, through the audience if possible, all rise to embrace loved ones. Bagpipers appear.

BOY, SHALLOW, BARDOLPH, PISTOL, DAVY, SOLDIERS
Come, let's away, …

The men raise colors and march off. The Falstaffians remain. Others enter and the enlistment cycle begins anew. Vendors and street entertainers join the scene. Exeunt soldiers with bagpipers.

SHALLOW, DAVY
… over the channel to France, boys!

SOLDIERS
Away, away, away!

DAVY
Take arms, lads! A guinea a man and a go at the French!

SHALLOW
Mark on the line! A guinea a man and a go at the French!

TOWNSWOMEN
Cider and vinegar, tuppence a pint!

TOWNSMEN
Who'll wrestle the Turk! A crown if you throw him!

SHALLOW
Join in, lads! A guinea a man, and a sail, boys!

DAVY
Join in lads! A walk in the sun and a sail, boys!

SHALLOW, DAVY, SOLDIERS
Shoulder your harness and shog, boys!

SHALLOW, DAVY, SOLDIERS AND TOWNSFOLK
Kiss her again and be off, boys! Good-bye to your girl and hello to the breach!

PISTOL
(*To Hostess*) My love, give me thy lips.

SOLDIERS
Form, lads!

TOWNSWOMEN
Apples and quince! Cider and vinegar! Apples and quince!

SOLDIERS
Kiss her again and be off, boys! Shoulder your harness and shog, boys!

TOWNSWOMEN
Cider and vinegar!

SOLDIERS
Kiss her again and away!

PISTOL
(*Sternly, to Hostess*) Look to my chattels and my movables.
Let senses rule: the word is 'Pitch and pay.'
Trust none; for oaths are straws, men's faiths are wafer cakes,
And Holdfast is the only dog, my duck.
Therefore Caveto be thy counselor. (*Hostess weeps.*)

SOLDIERS
Off to France! To France!

PISTOL
(*To Hostess, tenderly*) Go, clear thy crystals.

TOWNSWOMEN
Faith, lads, faith, lads!

A woman begins to dance. The men clap to the rhythm.

PISTOL
Yoke-fellows in arms, let us to France, like horse-leeches, my boys, to suck, to suck, the very blood to suck!

BOY, HOSTESS, SHALLOW, BARDOLPH, DAVY (Boy alone)
(*Amused at the hyperbole*) And that's but unwholesome food, they say.

BARDOLPH, PISTOL, DAVY
It's shoulder your pack. It's muster and march. It's follow the drum, ...

BOY, SHALLOW
Good-bye, Jane! Good-bye, Nan! Goodbye, Meg!

BOY, SHALLOW, BARDOLPH, PISTOL, DAVY, SOLDIERS AND TOWNSFOLK
… For the king's meat and the king's coin, and the king's true right!

Enter the King with Chief Justice and their train. All others fall to their knees, and priests give them absolution as before.

SOLDIERS AND TOWNSMEN
Deo gratias Anglia. Away.

TOWNSWOMEN
Away, away, away. (*As the train passes, all rise to say their last farewells.*) Man of arms, come safely, safely home.

PISTOL
Touch her soft mouth, and march.

Again bagpipers appear. The soldiers march off as before. The Falstaffians remain.

BOY, SHALLOW, BARDOLPH, DAVY, SOLDIERS AND TOWNSMEN
Come follow the colors and shog, my boys, come follow the colors and off, my boys, come step, lads, push, lads, march, lads! Come follow the pipes and away, my boys, and away. Good-bye, my love, bonjour, cherie, good-bye, my love, it's up with the anchor and over the sea! Come follow the pipes and away, my boys, and away, and away, and away!

The pipers and most of the soldiers are gone.

SOLDIERS
Away, away, away!

BOY (Bardolph)
Farewell, Hostess.

TOWNSWOMEN
Faith, lads!

BARDOLPH (Nym)
I cannot kiss, that is the humor of it; but adieu.

TOWNSWOMEN
Faith, lads!

PISTOL
Let housewifery appear. Keep close, I thee command.

All other men have now gone. The Falstaffian males join in the column. Lieutenant Pistol leads, Corporal Bardolph carries the colors and Boy beats the drum as they march off proudly for Southampton. The women remain.

SOLDIERS
(*Offstage*) March, boys! March, boys!

BOY, HOSTESS, TOWNSWOMEN
Farewell! Farewell!

SHALLOW, BARDOLPH, PISTOL, DAVY, SOLDIERS
March, lads! Fare thee well!

BOY, HOSTESS, TOWNSWOMEN
Adieu! Adieu!

SHALLOW, BARDOLPH, PISTOL, DAVY, SOLDIERS
March, lads! Fare thee well! Farewell! Farewell!

Curtain.

King Henry V at the siege of Harfleur 1415
Historical Images Archive / Alamy Stock Photo

USHER HOUSE

The Fall of the House of Usher • Walker Art Library

Usher House (Program Notes)

Poe's inter-grown house and family of Usher are artworks of morbidity and malaise worthy of the spectacular climax he devised for them. He has preferred to make mood everything, saving almost all dialogue and explicit action for the closing scene. There is no moral, no tragic flaw, no explanation. Poe rather gives us the logic of the nightmare, and on this plane his logic is airtight.

As this Gothic masterpiece reveals only glimpses of the plot, anyone who dramatizes it must work out the rest independently. *Usher House* quotes all the dialogue Poe gives us, as well as the opening and closing paragraphs of the story, and follows explicit events as far as we are told them. It otherwise takes liberties. To start, I make Poe himself the narrator who lives to tell the tale. More radically, I have conceived him and the doomed siblings as types of an antebellum warmth and gallantry which hardly exist anywhere in the prose of the real Poe, and must be counter to his purposes here. I have added other gothic staples—forbidden knowledge, a Faustian pact, ghostly ancestors—and have shifted all into a tale of good and evil and redemption. Good means Poe and the siblings, evil means Primus and the ancestors, and Madeline becomes the agent of redemption.

To fit this new design, I have played down Roderick's ailments, and played up his geniality and hospitality. I show no hint to his intolerance to light and noise, suggesting that the lumens and decibels that he meets are within his comfort zone, or, if not, that he is too considerate a host to wish to seem a burden. Meanwhile I have done everything I can to make Madeline endearing, not threatening. Only the forces of evil fear her. This premise can make the close all the more horrific.

Usher House (Synopsis)

<u>Prologue</u>

Georgia, around 1830. Projections show a dreary wasteland moving toward the audience, with Usher House coming into view at the end, as we hear Poe's voice quoting the first paragraph of the story.

<u>Scene 1</u>

Roderick greets his old school chum Poe at the door of his library, and leads him in as they share lively memories. Roderick has arranged a ball that night in Poe's honor. The other guests will all be family members who are old guests at Usher House. Poe guesses correctly that the house was built in Anglo-Saxon and Celtic times in Cornwall or Devon. Roderick shows him old references to it in books on his shelves. All warn of danger. *Exon Domesday Book* is quoted: Edward the Confessor had ordered Usher House to be torn apart, stone by stone, and the stones cast into a neighboring tarn. Both men laugh at such monkish superstition. Roderick confirms, however, that his father had drained the tarn, found the stones, and rebuilt the house in Georgia next to a tarn like the first.

A knock on the door. Enter Roderick's sister Madeline, mad and yet angelic, like Ophelia or Lucia, with her physician Primus. Both men have the breeding to notice nothing amiss. Poe had met her, still sane, when she had visited Roderick at school. Poe sings a song, "Where is my Lady?", which she had sung there to verse written by Poe and music composed by Roderick. Madeline and Primus leave. Roderick assures Poe that the medical knowledge stored in Usher House will restore her sanity. Then he collapses. He begs Poe to take her to Boston at daybreak, at Roderick's expense, to find a cure. Poe swears that he will. Another knock. The guests have arrived.

<u>Scene 2</u>

Roderick introduces Poe to the guests—Roderick's ghostly ancestors—at the ball. Aside, Poe reassures Roderick that he will keep his promise. Enter Madeline. The guests shrink back. She dances with Roderick, and then with Poe. Wilder music intervenes. She alone dances to it. She falls. Primus signs that she is dead.

Scene 3

Madeline's body is being deposited in the family crypt below Usher House. Roderick pays tribute. He reels, and is helped out. Primus tells Poe that a new line might have to be founded to save the archives of Usher House if Roderick were to die without issue. Poe, he implies, bears the qualities needed in such a new founder. Would Poe care to join him and the others at a meeting in the observatory the next evening to discuss matters further? Poe shares his concerns, but hesitates. Exit Primus. Poe, now alone, brushes dust off the inscriptions on the sepulchres lining the walls. He begins to read them. They give the names of guests he met at the ball. Last comes the name "Lord Primus Usher, Mortuit Anno 474."

Scene 4

Primus greets Poe as Poe enters the rooftop observatory the next evening. The guests from the ball are present. Primus recounts how generations of Ushers, under a covenant with the Elders of Avebury, had assembled medical archives since Roman times and before. The archives had to do with the delicate interchange between life and death. Some were destroyed by the Confessor, but the Ushers had gathered more. Now the stars revealed that great winds and great events will come in three nights. The Confessor's interdict will be expunged, the desecration avenged, the covenant glorified. Would Poe wish a share in these historic events? Again Poe hesitates.

Scene 5

Three nights have come. Poe paces nervously in Roderick's apartments. Roderick muses in an armchair. Poe reveals his meetings with Primus, and apologizes for not disclosing them sooner. Roderick accepts the apology, but remains distracted. Something vague is troubling him. He asks Poe to read out some frivolous text to help him look at things anew. Poe pulls down a book of hyperbolic knightly valor, and begins. As the story describes the rending of planks and a dragon's roar, and the ringing of a falling shield, we hear such sounds in the distance.

Roderick raises his hand. He has solved his puzzle. The first sound was of Madeline rending her coffin and vault. The second was Primus' cry as she cast him aside. The third was of her breaking down the door to the great hall, which the ancestors had barricaded against her. Now she approaches the steps to this chamber. She comes to complete the work of the Confessor. We hear her singing the melody of "Where is my Lady?" wordlessly as she climbs the stairs. She enters. Brother and sister rush into each other's arms. They fall dead. Poe escapes.

Epilogue

Projections show Usher House collapsing into the tarn in a lightning storm as we hear Poe's voice quoting the last paragraph of the story.

The Fall of the House of Usher
Lebrecht Music & Arts / Alamy Stock Photo

USHER HOUSE
Opera in One Act

Libretto
By Gordon Getty
2008

after

The Fall of the House of Usher
By Edgar Allan Poe

Cast of Characters in Order of Appearance

Edgar Allan POE
RODERICK Usher, Poe's host and old friend
MADELINE Usher, Roderick's sister
Doctor PRIMUS[116], Madeline's physician
ATTENDANT

NOTE: Text with a solid line in the left margin indicates original source material. Text with a dot in the left margin indicates adapted source material.

Prologue

A soft light flickers equally over the sides and front of the auditorium. Scrim depicts a miasmic swampland, moving toward the audience as if seen by a traveler. The voice of Poe is heard from no place in particular.

POE
During the whole of a dull, dark and soundless day, in the autumn of the year, when the clouds hung oppressively low in the heavens, I had been passing alone, on horseback, through a singularly dreary tract of country, and at length, found myself, as the shades of evening drew on, within view of the melancholy House of Usher.

---

[116] Pronounced "PREE-mus"

Scene 1

Glimmering light out. Lights up on Roderick leading Poe into the library.

RODERICK
Can it be five years, my friend? Is it possible, Eddie?

POE
Roderick, upon my word, it is.

RODERICK
Is it possible? Five years! I fear that time has not noticed us here in our solitary world. Our clocks are the seasons; they run slow. But you will enliven us. What is the news of Richmond, Boston, London? And what of our classmates? Do you still hear from Crewe? Has Stone found enough to eat? And what of good Professor Grubbins? Dr. Dodge? They will not have forgotten such a scholar as Eddie Poe! (*Motions him to sit. They sit.*)

POE
(*Laughing*) All of them well, Roderick. In the pink. Crewe married Ellen, and Stone is fatter than ever. But I, a scholar? A poor counterfeit, to any that had known Roderick Usher for comparison.

RODERICK
Nonsense!

POE
Yes, they knew better.

RODERICK
Nonsense!

POE
You were the real article.

RODERICK
Nonsense!

POE

Mine was the dunce cap, as between us two. Yours were the laurels.

RODERICK

Not a bit! None could touch you! (*Both men laugh heartily.*) And it is not five years! (*Sobering*) Yet I know, well I know, my friend, that every day of them must show in my appearance. Let us speak plainly. You see that my letter did not exaggerate. I hope you are not distressed. Yes, my old disorders have worsened. I have become quite sensitive to sound and light. I fear our old revels and carousals would be quite beyond me. (*Brightening again*) But that does not mean that hospitality has left Usher House! Indeed, we have arranged a surprise tonight in your honor! I will hear no protest!

POE

A surprise? (*Laughing*) Roderick, you put me up to your old puzzles.

RODERICK

No puzzles, Eddie! I have learned my lesson many times. Nothing can be hidden from Eddie Poe. (*Both men laugh.*) I will reveal everything in a moment. But first, tell me, Eddie, have we provided well for you? Are your rooms comfortable? Are you rested and refreshed? I trust we have not disgraced ourselves. Guests are valued here, and scholars above all. If you are tired from your journey, then say but a word, and the surprise can be put off.

POE

Tired? Not in the least! From Savannah to Poole's Landing by comfortable packet this morning, then the ride here through your picturesque marshland. A few easy hours.

RODERICK

Eddie, the truth!

POE

I swear it, Roderick! I have never felt fresher. And as for puzzles, I could never learn a fraction of your skill in them. You are still a legend at school. Do you know that you solve mysteries in my stories, under another name?

RODERICK

Eddie, what an honor!

POE

You review famous crimes in Paris from news accounts, after the Prefecture gives them up as insoluble, and solve them while scarcely stirring from your chair. None who know you will doubt that I mean Roderick Usher. But my stories are only sketches now. They will go no further without your blessing.

RODERICK

Then you have it! Stories about me by Eddie Poe! That will put some shine on the family crest! I cannot wait to read them! But Eddie, I have still said nothing about the surprise tonight.

POE

You have not, my old friend, and you must now have pity on me. I fear I am still a child at heart. Reveal the surprise!

RODERICK

Well then, we shall have a ball! Nothing less will do! A ball, this very night! All our guests have been avid to meet the famous man of letters. I have written some pieces for it myself, just as in the old days. You shall judge if they are worth hearing. If not, have no mercy!

POE

New music by Roderick Usher would have brought me here at a gallop, even if our old friendship were not reason enough!

RODERICK

Done, then! We shall have a ball!

POE

Done! But the guests, Roderick. Where have you found them? From landfall onward, I saw not a single person nor habitation. Do they somehow come from Savannah? Or (*In jest*) do you summon them up from the depths, like a sorcerer?

RODERICK

(*With only a moment of embarrassment*) Just so, my friend! Just so, in a way. They come from the depths of this house, and before that from Savannah and very much farther. Each of them is an old visitor here. Usher House is indeed remote. And you are too kind as to our landscape. It is desolate. But we have rooms aplenty and a devotion to family. Many of my relatives share this roof. You will meet them tonight. I hope we will not disappoint you with our musty ways. We are not as modish[117] as those of the great cities. But there are lovers of learning among us.

POE
Perfect! I come here to cleanse myself of the modishness of the great cities. I welcome the lovers of learning!

RODERICK[118]
Then you will be at home in Usher House. I do not boast. Scholars here have never been disappointed in their welcome or in our resources. We Ushers have always been devoted to the old studies, every one of us, from father to son beyond remembrance. And we are a race of collectors. We have spared no pains, no expense. We have brought together tracts, monographs, manuscripts of the greatest interest and rarity. Come, Eddie, first let us look at some of our old favorites! (*Both men rise.*) Here are manuscripts of Gresset[119], Swedenborg[120], the *Belphegor*[121] of Machiavelli, the *Directory of the Inquisition* by Eymeric[122] de Gironne[123], and look here, Eddie! Here is the *Vigiliae Mortuorum*. Yes, it exists after all! All these but whet the appetite. Pride of place belongs to our medical archives. The ancients knew secrets that would astound the schools today. We have threshed out many of them, and will more. The whole house is designed for learning. Soon we will show you our observatory, where anyone who likes can study the stars in the old manner. Have I told you of the history of Usher House?

POE
Roderick, you have not, but let me guess a little.

RODERICK
By all means!

---

[117] Pronounced "MOW-dish"
[118] All books mentioned by Roderick in this passage are named in the story.
[119] Pronounced "GRES-SAY"
[120] Pronounced "SWEE-duhn-borg"
[121] Pronounced "BEL-feh-gohr"
[122] Pronounced "EH-mer-ik"
[123] Pronounced "duh jhee-ROHN"

POE
Apart from the modern conveniences, I should have said it was Anglo-Saxon, even partly Celtic.[124] And mightn't it be more at home in the moors of Devon or Cornwall than here in sultry Georgia?

RODERICK
Bravo, exact! I knew you would not disappoint me. It was built long before the Conquest. None of us is certain when. It stood on the ancestral land of the Ushers, near Exeter. Gildas writes of it.

POE
Gildas!

RODERICK
Yes, parts of it are very old indeed. He writes of a shrine at Usher-on-Exe. It would have been pagan, but we cannot be sure to what god. The *Anglo-Saxon Chronicles* are silent, but there is a most lurid entry in *Doomsday Book*. I warn you, they are not flattering. (*Amused*) This is Bede[125]: "a heterodox monastery at Usher on Exe avoided by the countryfolk." And Dunstan: (*Reading, hamming it up derisively*) "A great keep, minster and library by Usher Tarn, but of poor reputation." (*Both men laugh.*) Unflattering, to be sure! But let us not make too much of the pious caveats of Dunstan or Bede. Dogma, dogma was the thing, and men saw devils in the slightest inconformance.

POE
And what of *Exon Doomsday*?

RODERICK
I have saved that for last. It tells of the most bizarre and ignominious episode in our long history. (*Shows Poe the passage.*) I will let you read it without further preface by me.

Poe reads silently.

POE
(*Speaking*) Good God!

---

[124] Pronounced "Seltic"
[125] Pronounced "Beed"

RODERICK

(*From memory*) "Atque idem"... no, it is better in English: "and King Edward the Confessor commanded that the building called Usher House be sundered stone from stone, and the stones cast into Usher Tarn." Into the tarn, no less! We can but guess at the cause of the Confessor's wrath. Yet as late as my father's time, the yeomanry there claimed that lightning from the skies clove the house in two. It is a district famous for its legends. (*Both men chuckle.*) But the stones were indeed there at the bottom of Usher Tarn, when my father bought back the land and drained it. He hauled them here and rebuilt Usher House, with modern conveniences, over a tarn as like the first as he could find, even as to the faint phosphorescence that you will have noticed on your approach. He even brought back the crypt, which the Confessor had spared. And apart from the usual problems of settling, as you will have seen in the faint crack running down the keep, tradition has been restored as far as the skill of the artisans would permit. We are a stubborn race, and one not content with the verdict of the Confessor. Ushers homeless for centuries gathered here with their hoarded volumes. No, we are not content that the learning of Usher House should be cast into the tarn!

USHER HOUSE, December 8, 2023
Digital Painting in Photoshop using Wakom Tablet and pen. 12" x 17"
© Nicolette Beck

POE
(*Singing*) Nor am I content! (*Sits.*) We resolved once, you and I, never to flinch from knowledge. I have kept that promise.

RODERICK
And I. It is an Usher trait. And we revere this house. We travel wherever the old learning can be found, but we come home to die. Even during our Diaspora, when nothing but the crypt remained, Ushers gathered here to commemorate, and were buried here. To Ushers, we and this house and the knowledge are one. Eddie, Eddie, this house was built by Ushers in the morning of the world, crafted of stone and time and wisdom, when learning too could build until it fell, before saints and psalms and Caesars drove it under. We have found almost all, shred and shard, the ancient light, the wisdom unafraid, and will piece it together. Enough may be already here, Eddie, not all, but enough. Who masters it can master the world, Eddie; he can tether the seas and the stars! We Ushers have hunted for knowledge wherever it hides, from pole to pole, wherever saints and Caesars drove it, and we may have enough. A little more study, Eddie, a little more reflection, and we will ride on the wind, Eddie, we will build on the seas, we will muster and master the stars!

POE
Then let me join in the hunt!

RODERICK
Willingly! We will hunt the fox to earth! But there are dangers in the hunt. We know them. We respect them. Bede and Dunstan spoke the truth. The heterodox are avoided. Yes, it is laughable, but it is true, even now. There is danger in learning, even now.

There is a knock at the door. Roderick has time for a look of anxiety and gesture of caution to Poe before Madeline and Primus enter. Roderick and Poe rise.

RODERICK
Dear Madeline! Eddie, you will remember my sister Madeline when she visited me at school. We were only children then, the three of us, and now look how beautiful she has become!

Madeline gazes vacantly ahead in the serenity of madness.

POE
Miss Madeline, I am more than honored to renew our acquaintance. I look forward to the pleasure of your company during my visit here.

Both men have the breeding to pretend to notice nothing strange.

RODERICK
And may I introduce you to Dr. Primus? Dr. Primus, my old friend Edgar Poe of Richmond.

POE
It is my pleasure, sir.

PRIMUS
And mine, Mr. Poe. Your fame in the old studies has reached us all. But now I fear Miss Madeline must take her medicine and prepare for bed. She is getting so much better, and we must not interrupt her recovery.

RODERICK
(*Nods.*) And Dr. Primus, would you care to join us for a moment, as soon as your duties permit?

PRIMUS
Certainly.

Primus leads Madeline toward the door. Halfway there, she turns. She runs to Roderick and embraces him. She then gives her hand to Poe. He kisses it. She turns again, then walks back to Primus, who resumes leading her out. Exeunt Madeline and Primus. Poe starts to say something, but Roderick again catches him with a gesture. Primus re-enters.

RODERICK
(*To Poe*) Now you have seen her. This is the sorrow of which my letter spoke.

POE
My friend, I did not know. I grieve with you. Yet she is perfect. I grieve with you and envy you. And yes, Roderick, I remember her visit at school. You may recall some lines I wrote then, and how beautifully she sang your setting of them.

RODERICK
I do.

POE
    "Where is my lady, O where has she gone?
    Over the moonrise and over the dawn.
    Follow her easterly, follow the trace
    Of her toe on the wind; she has run to the place
    Where the morning begins, and the sea, and the sky.
    Beauty and grace she is; beauty and grace
    Hang in the air like chimes where she goes by.

    What if I follow as best I can try,
    And ring the wide world, and yet fail in the chase?
    Follow her southerly; follow the mark
    Of her foot in the light, of her foot in the dark,
    Easterly, southerly, follow the train
    Where she runs in the starlight, she runs in the rain,
    In footfall and starfall, again and again.
    Beauty and grace she is; beauty and grace
    Hang in the air like chimes where she goes by."

She was my model in writing that. It is as true of her now as then. Over and over I hear those lines, and I think I shall hear them for some time to come. Roderick, she is so delicate, so pure!

RODERICK
"Beauty and grace"! Yes, that is Madeline. You saw the truth, as always. Yet she is not so frail as one would suppose. In her catalepsy she might even be capable of great strength. Is it not so, Dr. Primus?

PRIMUS
It is so. Prolonged excitement could give her more strength than one would have thought possible.

RODERICK
We are fortunate to have Dr. Primus with us, and to manage the scholarly resources of this house. I spoke of our medical archives. Now you see why

they are vital to me. A cure will be found. Madeline's case is not hopeless. We will restore her health. We will cure my sister. Will we not, Dr. Primus?

PRIMUS
Every treatment is being applied ... consistent with her tolerance for it.

Roderick throws him an uneasy glance, but Primus stares ahead.

RODERICK
My sister will recover. I am certain of it. Now, Dr. Primus, we must not keep you from your patient. My friend and I have many old recollections to share.

PRIMUS
Of course. (*Exit Primus.*)

RODERICK
Her mind is serene and pure. Many of us could envy her that. I would not deprive her of it, not for everything else in the world.

POE
She is an angel. Had I the power, I would not dare to change her.

RODERICK
Wisely spoken. Yet I would give her an ordinary life if I could. A cure can be found. It must be found! The learning of this house is equal to the task. If we bring it all to bear, encompass it all… (*Roderick breaks into sobs.*) My sister, my sister! We are twins, you know. We were children of one soul. I knew her thoughts, and she mine. When she cried in the dark, I would comfort her … I would comfort her …

MADELINE as a CHILD
(*In Roderick's memory*)
Roderick, I am cold. I am afraid.

RODERICK
I would comfort her.

RODERICK as a CHILD
Madeline, sister, I will comfort you.

MADELINE as a CHILD
Roderick, Roderick, it is dark here.

RODERICK
I would comfort her. Madeline!

RODERICK as a CHILD
Madeline, sister, I am here by the window.

RODERICK
Madeline!

RODERICK as a CHILD
I am here in the starlight.

RODERICK
Madeline, Madeline! (*More sobs. Then he becomes anxious, agitated, intense. He draws closer to Poe as if to baffle an eavesdropper.*) Edgar, can you take her from here? For pity's sake, take her away. Conditions here are not best for her. Leave at daybreak, the two of you. Take the noon packet to Boston. Secure the best doctors, place her in the best clinics. I will provide everything. I have not the strength, and my eyes could not tolerate the sunlight. Do it at daybreak, for mercy's sake. Swear that you will!

POE
(*Amazed at this volte-face, but moved*) I will, my friend. I swear that I will do it.

Roderick grips his hand. Another knock at the door. Poe opens it, listens to someone outside.

POE
(*To Roderick*) The guests have arrived.

Lights out.

Scene 2

The Great Hall, decked out as a ballroom. Roderick and Poe stand together, and Primus nearby. Musicians play. Ancestors are dancing. Others enter and are announced by the Attendant. They then bow or curtsy to Roderick as master of the house, then to Poe as guest of honor, and then join the dancers.

ATTENDANT
Lady Heliane Usher and Lord Pengarth Usher of Exeter … Mrs. Oliver Usher of Swansea and Mr. Hamish Usher of Philadelphia …

RODERICK
I hope you will find some interest in the costumes. They recapitulate the family history. Ushers are here from many places, many times.

ATTENDANT
Lord Mordoc, Thane of Usher and the Lady Berenice …

After these last two greet Roderick and Poe, as before, Primus escorts them silently to Lord Pengarth and Lady Heliane at a distant part of the stage. As soon as Primus is out of earshot, Roderick takes Poe's arm and speaks quickly, quietly.

RODERICK
(*To Poe*) At daybreak?

POE
(*To Roderick*) At daybreak. I will not sleep.

ATTENDANT
Miss Hannah Usher and her brother, The Honorable Eldred Usher, both of Drogheda[126] …

By the time these two have finished greeting Roderick and Poe, Primus has returned.

RODERICK
(*To Poe, but for Primus' benefit*) So you see, my old friend, we are not so provincial after all.

Again, Primus moves away to other guests.

---

[126] Pronounced "DROY-da"

RODERICK
(*To Poe*) At daybreak?

POE
(*To Roderick*) At daybreak.

ATTENDANT
(*Stentorian*) Dr. and Mrs. Duncan Usher, of Agra. His Excellency, Count Leopold Usher and Countess Melanie Usher of …

Enter Madeline. The Ancestors shrink against the walls in terror, as vampires from a crucifix. She curtsies to Roderick, then gives Poe a flower. Madeline dances with Roderick. The Ancestors clap soundlessly. Then Madeline dances with Poe as the musicians play "Ewig Du." The Ancestors join Poe and Madeline in the dance. Wilder dance music is heard with "Ewig Du," and then alone. Madeline pauses, confused. So do Poe and the Ancestors. Madeline begins again, and all resume. Only Madeline and the audience hear the new music, and she alone dances to it. Musicians continue visibly playing, and Ancestors dancing, to the tempo of "Ewig Du." Poe stops, perplexed. Now all notice Madeline. Musicians stop playing. Ancestors retreat to watch. Madeline seems dazed. The Ancestors take a step toward Madeline. Another step. They continue. Madeline falls. Primus indicates that she is dead. Roderick collapses in grief. Poe consoles him. Lights out.

Scene 3

We are at Madeline's burial in the crypt below the keep. Vaults with inscriptions appear on the walls. Roderick, Poe, Primus and the Ancestors are present. The coffin is ready to be deposited.

RODERICK
And now it is time to bid our silent farewells to my sister Madeline. She brought us the springtime, and we will have its memory forever.

The coffin is deposited and the vault sealed. Roderick reels, then catches himself. Some of the Ancestors help him out of the crypt. Poe, Primus and the other Ancestors remain.

PRIMUS
(*To all present, but particularly to Poe*) I fear the master of the house may not long outlive the mistress. If the line of the Ushers were no more, its libraries and scholars might be scattered, its traditions unhoused. What might be done to keep it all intact? There must be new leadership once the line is ended. An exemplary scholar, young, vital, a friend to the Ushers, might advise us. For perpetuity's sake, a new line might need to be founded. If our guest cares to consider these matters and share his thoughts with us, he may wish to visit us in the observatory tomorrow evening. Now we may leave him, if he prefers, to pay his respects in private.

POE
I will reflect. To the devoted student, Usher House is a paradigm, a pinnacle. It must not be lost. But there are solemn questions to be asked. I will remain here for a moment.

Exeunt Primus and the Ancestors.

POE
(*Speaking toward Madeline's vault*)
    "Beauty and grace she is, beauty and grace
    Hang in the air like chimes where she goes by."

Thank you, Miss Madeline, for a moment of solace in a troubled world.

He places the flower she had given him before the vault. He turns to leave, but his eye catches something in the inscriptions on the other vaults. He wipes away some dust and brings his candelabra closer. He repeats the sequence along the front of the stage, which the audience interprets as the fourth wall.

POE
(*Reading aloud from the inscriptions*) "Lord Mordoc and Lady Berenice Usher … Eldred Usher … Hannah … Hamish … Lord Pengarth and Lady Heliane … (*He rubs away more dust.*) … Lord Primus Usher, *mortuit anno* 474."

He steps back in wonderment. Lights fade out slowly.

Scene 4

We are in the rooftop observatory in a night full of stars. The Ancestors are present. Primus is greeting Poe as he enters from a stairwell.

PRIMUS
We are particularly honored to receive our guest here in the observatory. Ushers have studied the stars for centuries. The heavens are books for the literate to read. Much, much can be foreseen. For example, we know that unusual weather phenomena will center on this place three nights hence.

POE
Weather? Of what kind?

PRIMUS
There will be great winds, and more than winds. But let us come to that in due course. First, we must make certain we are not pressing unwelcome topics. Investigation is not without cost. There is knowledge that many find distressing. Is our guest quite certain he wishes to hear more?

POE
I am a student. All knowledge is welcome to me.

PRIMUS
Then let us go a little further. First, you are modest. Your work is esteemed here. Few have looked so deeply into the shadows. Few have stepped so far along the passages that lead into this life, and from it. We know from your work that you can be trusted to see and trusted to comprehend. That is why we expect you to have found matters of antiquarian interest yesterday, when left in private after the ensepulchre of the Lady Madeline.

POE
I did so.

PRIMUS
All of us bear ancient names. Their recurrence is a tradition here. On the other hand, more than names can be passed from the dead to the living. More than names endure. You have heard something of our medical archives. The knowledge in them extends to a deeper understanding of life and death.

Life and death, their delicate interchange, their gradations, can be whatever medical science makes of them. The magisters of Egypt and Anatolia and Brittany had learned these things over the millennia. Roman law opposed the knowledge, and so then did Church law. All was destroyed, or hidden. Some was granted to us, and to us alone, under a covenant with the Elders of Avebury. More was obtained from the Hierarch of Syracuse and from other royal and private collections. This was passed on to Ushers with the will and aptitude to learn it. The lady Madeline has been recusant. She refused the knowledge and accepted the common path. The master of the house wavers. If Usher tradition could be grafted onto new roots, then the new line would inherit all the knowledge. This, of course, would include the proprietary medical skills of which we have been speaking. Would our guest care to hear more?

POE
I am afraid. But I have sworn to follow knowledge to the limits of my reach. I will hear more.

PRIMUS
Then we can meet again three nights from this. Conditions will be fitter then. You will have noticed the haze or miasma that rises from the tarn and enfolds this house, though the dull might have missed it. It has to do with the medical matters of which we spoke. We call it the illumination. It had been present at the old site, in England, but the powers of the Confessor had dispersed it. Now we have found it again. In three days' time it will flame to a grandeur not seen in many lifetimes. Through its force, the interdict of the Confessor will be expunged, the desecration avenged, the wisdom promulgated, the covenant glorified. Does our guest wish to share in these historic events?

POE
I am afraid. But I have sworn never to turn aside from knowledge. I will reflect.

Lights out.

Scene 5

Three nights have passed. We are in Roderick's apartments. Outside, the storm that had been forecast is stirring. Roderick sits deep in thought. Poe paces nervously.

POE
Roderick, I must speak. I have heard things that I must not keep from you. Doctor Primus has spoken to me in the presence of the others. I believe they would make me heir to the secrets of this house. For the first time, I am afraid of this knowledge. My friend, forgive me for listening without your permission, and for delaying this report.

RODERICK
I knew or guessed it from the start, and you are forgiven. You have spoken honestly. But beware of Primus. Did he speak of the importance of this night?

POE
He said that the winds would rise. The phosphorescence from the tarn, or illumination as he called it, would glow bright. It had to do with the secrets of life and death. The Confessor's interdict would be expunged, and the covenant glorified.

RODERICK
(*Musing*) So he said even that. It is All-Hallows' Eve. And it was All-Hallows' Eve eight centuries ago when the Confessor defied the powers of that night and brought down this house. It was Primus Usher who made the covenant with the Elders, fourteen centuries ago, and founded our line by Usher Tarn. That line is nearly extinct. I say it frankly. And Primus Usher must settle his account. Primus knows that, and fears.

POE
Roderick, in the name of sanity, can that Primus Usher and this one be the same?

RODERICK
He will have told you the answer to that, in riddles. And he will have spoken of dangers in pressing further. Let us respect the dangers, and leave the riddles as they are. No doubt he will renew the debt if he can, substituting your line

for mine. But Primus is deep and wise. He must have another plan, one that would keep the original pact in force.

POE
My true friend, there will be no substitution of lines. I repent my folly in hearing such a proposal. The debt will not be renewed.

RODERICK
I trust and believe you. Those same follies were once my own. I will pay for them. Still, Primus must have a plan. He is desperate or confident. Else he would not have dared to tell you so much, little as it is. He has placed himself in jeopardy. He has a plan. We ourselves may be at risk if we cannot puzzle it out. (*Short pause.*) But there is something else that weighs on me. It is an anxiety, a dread, whose occasion I cannot fix in my mind. Something frightful, something hideous and insupportable remains at the border of my gaze wherever I turn. It has obsessed me for hours, even days. I cannot find it, I cannot escape it. Surely you have seen this, and have been too kind to speak.

POE
I have seen it, but thought the fault was mine. I should never have countenanced these intrigues. You guessed them. That was the seed of your foreboding, or its nourishment. Perhaps it would be best if I withdrew to my room, and wronged my friend no further.

RODERICK
No, Edgar, stay. For God's sake, stay. You are guiltless. The cause, whatever it is, is not in you. For our old friendship, stay and help me now. Somewhere I have overlooked a warning, or left an obligation in suspense. Now the winds are rising. Primus will set his plan in motion soon. We must find it out. I must think. Yet my other apprehension distracts me.

POE
Then let me help if I can.

RODERICK
Could you read something aloud to me? You recall that at school, when I had undertaken a problem in philosophy or the calculus whose answer did not come readily, I sometimes preferred to weigh it in the midst of conversation,

or even on the sporting field, rather than in the quiet of my rooms. Often you were present, and were the first hearer of my proposed solution, once I had struck on it, before any save possibly yourself could have guessed that a problem had occupied me. It is so now. Silence torments me. Read, read aloud. Something trivial, diverting. Let us banish silence and sober thought for the moment, in hope of looking at things anew.

Poe rapidly scans the shelves and pulls down a volume.

POE[127]
This may do. It is the *Mad Tryst* of Sir Launcelot Channing.

RODERICK
(*Claps hands and laughs merrily.*) Excellent! Give us, if you will, the part where our knight breaks into the hermit's house.

POE
Let me have a moment. (*Finds the page, then hams up his recitation to spoof the purple prose.*)

> "And Ethelred, who was by nature of a doughty heart, waited no longer to hold parley with the hermit, but fearing the rising of the tempest, uplifted his mace and, with blows, made quickly room in the plankings of the door for his gauntleted hand, and so cracked, and ripped, and tore all asunder that the noise alarumed and reverberated throughout the forest.

A faint sound of this description has been heard as Poe concludes. Poe is startled. Roderick remains deep in thought.

> "But the good champion Ethelred, now entering the door, was sore amazed to perceive a dragon of a scaly and prodigious demeanor. And Ethelred uplifted his mace and struck the dragon, which fell before him with a shriek so horrid and harsh, and withal so piercing, that Ethelred had fain to close his ears with his hands against the dreadful noise of it.

---

[127] The title and author are as in the original.

Some such sound has been heard as before. Again Poe reacts while Roderick stares straight ahead.

> "And now the champion, bethinking himself of the brazen shield, approached valorously over the silver pavement of the castle to where it hung upon the wall, which in sooth tarried not for his full coming, but fell down at his feet upon the silver floor, with a mighty, great and terrible ringing sound."

Once again such a sound has been heard, still faintly. Poe reacts more strongly and is about to comment, but Roderick raises his hand.

RODERICK
Yes, I have heard it. I heard its faint beginnings four nights ago, through wood and stone. Go from this house, my friend. You know how painfully keen my hearing has become. I can hear the fluttering of the moth's wings, the fall of leaves in the woods. Go, my friend. I and this house will close our business very soon. Go now, and no harm will come to you.

POE
I will not leave you in danger.

RODERICK
I say, I heard it that first night.

MADELINE as a CHILD
Roderick, brother, it is dark here.

RODERICK
It was she. I heard her stirring in her prison. She cried out to me in the dark, and I did not comfort her. I did not understand.

RODERICK as a CHILD
Madeline, come to the window. Come to the starlight. I will comfort you.

RODERICK
She was never of their circle, never. But what vows might she not have taken in her despair?

Madeline as an adult, offstage, pure and childlike, begins singing the melody of "Where is my Lady" on the vowel "ah."

RODERICK
(*As Madeline sings*) And might I not, if she had done? There has never been a plan more ingenious, more heinous or more pitiless. I tell you, he has dared to open the roof portals, even on this night. He has brought the illumination into this house. Look! (*Roderick rises and opens the door to the corridor. The "illumination" is everywhere.*) I say, he would have invited the Elders themselves, had he now the power. He would have delivered the three of us, healthy as colts, scion and all, the line and the bargain intact. (*Roderick closes the door.*) Now go, Edgar. Go at once!

POE
My friend, Primus shall face the both of us or neither.

RODERICK
(*Laughing*) Primus! Primus and his plan are in ruins. He confronted her in the armory below, as you were reading. She threw him aside like an empty sack. She is still pure. He was powerless before her. She made no vows in the dark.

Madeline's voice is heard again offstage, singing continuously as she approaches.

The writ of the Confessor runs still. It has sustained her in her madness. She comes to complete his work. Run, my friend! The rest of us have only a few more moments. My penance will be short and blithe compared to theirs.

MADELINE as a CHILD
Roderick, it is dark. I am afraid.

RODERICK
You are free. In God's name, go!

RODERICK as a CHILD
Madeline, sister, I will comfort you.

RODERICK
As you recited, we both heard first the rending of her coffin and vault. I have said she has the strength of many men. Then we heard the cry of Primus as she discarded him. Last we heard her break down the doors of the great hall, which the others had barricaded against her. But she has no interest in them. As we speak, she ascends the steps leading to this chamber.

RODERICK as a CHILD
Madeline …

MADELINE as a CHILD
Roderick …

RODERICK[128]
Escape by the side passage, my friend. Listen! The stones! Hear them! She is throwing them into the tarn! Sister, I am here! I will comfort you! Madman, madman, I tell you, she now stands without the door!

The doors are blown open by the storm. Lights out, except for the "illumination" streaming in from the doorway. Madeline stands there in her cerements, then runs to Roderick. They embrace and fall dead. The house is heard more than seen to collapse. It does so in the darkness except for quick flashes of light and the "illumination" centering on Roderick and Madeline. Poe has fled unseen. As the commotion dies down, we hear the unlocalized voice of Poe as before.

POE
From that chamber, and from that mansion, I fled aghast. I saw the mighty walls rushing asunder, and the deep and dark tarn at my feet closing sullenly and silently over the fragments of the House of Usher.

Curtain.

---

[128] Roderick's final sentence here quotes Poe.

THE CANTERVILLE GHOST

Sir Simon and The Twins: Illustration from The Canterville Ghost • Evgenija Chistotina

The Canterville Ghost (Program Notes)

Wilde's finest poetry is in his prose, and his finest prose is in his children's stories. Most are dark. Sacrifice and heartbreak are the themes. Frank homage is paid to Hans Christian Andersen, whose little match girl and little mermaid repeat their roles in Wilde's *The Happy Prince* and *The Fisherman and His Soul*.

The Canterville Ghost looks at the sunnier side. Virginia's sacrifice, and the ghost's remorse, reach the endings we hoped for. All of Wilde's ideas but one are inspired. He was never in better form. Not many writers could have sent up the stolid Otises or the indignant Sir Simon so richly while leaving us on their side throughout.

While *Usher House* turns Poe upside down, the libretto for *The Canterville Ghost* follows Wilde's short story pretty closely. His one misjudgment was Sir Simon's murder of his wife, three centuries before, and his breezy justification of it to Virginia. That might have fit in many of Wilde's works. Here it grates against the wholesome and family-friendly theme. The libretto, like the 1944 movie with Charles Laughton, changes this detail. The bloodstain is also relocated from the floor to the armor, so that the audience can see it. Also, Canterville and Cheshire are given more continuous roles, Washington Otis is left out, and Mrs. Umney is seen but not heard. These changes reflect no critique of Wilde. Stage and page have different needs.

The fidelity of the libretto to the original, these aside, led to twenty scenes averaging three minutes. These quick changes call for high-tech staging, with a minimum of bulk to haul on and off. A two-level set to distinguish bedrooms from the dining room and library should be considered, but not necessarily preferred. Any such structure would have to be able to retract quickly and silently for the outdoor scenes.

When *Usher House* and *Canterville* are staged as a double bill, or even separately, it is probably more effective to show the ancestors in the first, and most or all nonspeaking clambake guests in the second, as projections. This is all the more advantageous in that the ancestors must dance and the guests play sports. The time is past when actual performers, however adept, are likely to work well at this within limits of time and space and budget. The staff in *Canterville* should be real actors, even so, as we want no suggestion that they are supernatural. They can double as family members in Scene 1, with a quick change to get them to the start of Scene 2.

Wilde's story has Sir Simon fall down the stairs once to escape the twins. Now I have him falling down the stairs at the end of every scene with them. Think of him as Wile E. Coyote, the twins as two Road Runners, and the stairs as the rim of the Grand Canyon. The key is to make it funny every time by incorporating new twists that somehow capitalize on the fact that the audience sees it coming, and by remembering that nothing is funny if it actually seems to harm. Remember also that the Road Runner never intends Wile E. Coyote to fall off the rim. Laughter could be uncomfortable if he did. An impression of innocent fun is vital.

The opera, like the story, is romantic comedy. It doesn't play if it doesn't make us laugh and cry in the right places in the right way, and to sympathize with all the characters throughout.

The Canterville Ghost (Synopsis)

Scene 1

Virginia and Cheshire, now old, are surrounded by three generations of descendants at Sir Simon's gravesite. They explain to the youngest ones that Sir Simon was really a ghost, and that Virginia, seventy years before, had led him to peace.

Scene 2

We are at Canterville Chase seventy years earlier. Canterville welcomes the Otis family, who have just bought the Chase from him, and warns them about the ghost of Sir Simon. Their twin sons take the news with glee, their daughter Virginia with sympathy for the ghost, and they themselves with Yankee aplomb. Mrs. Otis notices a red stain on a suit of armor upstage. Canterville explains that it is the blood of Sir Simon's brother-in-law, murdered by him on the spot three centuries before. The stain cannot be removed. "Nonsense!" proclaims Otis. He produces a jar of Pinkerton's Champion Stain Remover, and scrubs the stain away. Thunder and lightning. Otis remarks on the English weather. Canterville invites all to call him in case of need, and takes his leave.

Scene 3

The family comes down to the same room three mornings later. The stain has reappeared, after being scrubbed away, for three days in a row—and twice with the door locked in between. Mrs. Otis opines that it might be the ghost after all. Otis agrees, and suggests that it would be only fair for the ghost to pay them rent. He will write a letter to the firm of Myers and Padmore on the matter, and draft an article on the Permanence of Sanguinous Stains when Connected to Crime. All proceed to breakfast.

Scene 4

Midnight in an upstairs corridor. Moaning and clanking of chains. Enter the ghost as he drags the chains to the door of the master bedroom. Otis opens the door, and insists politely that the ghost must oil his chains, as sleep would otherwise be impossible. He gives the ghost a bottle of the Tammany Rising

Sun Lubricator for that purpose, and closes the door. The ghost, howling with indignation, dashes the bottle to the floor, and lurches back the way he came. The twins emerge, and whiz pillows past his head. He flees, and tumbles down the stairs as they jump up and down.

Scene 5

The ghost, in his room immediately after, rages against the Otises, lists his artistic triumphs in terrifying the high and mighty over three centuries, and vows revenge.

Scene 6

All are at breakfast next morning in the dining room. Otis is disappointed that the ghost has not accepted the lubricator. The firm of Myers and Padmore has assured him that if the ghost does not oil his chains, Otis would be quite justified in taking them from him, or in proceeding with eviction on ground of nuisance, as well as non-payment of rent. He hopes that this step will not be necessary, considering the ghost's long residence in the house, and chides the twins, to their merriment, for throwing pillows at his head. Mrs. Otis agrees.

Scene 7

Midnight in the upstairs corridor again. Enter the ghost, moaning as before, but this time wearing the suit of armor rather than the chains as he shambles to the door. This time it is Mrs. Otis who opens it. If his problem is indigestion, as she fears, the ghost will find Dr. Dobell's Tincture an excellent remedy; performing artists such as himself owe the public due attention to their health. She hands him a phial of the tincture, and closes the door. The twins ambush him with pea-shooters as he retreats, and he tumbles down the stairs as before.

Scene 8

Again the ghost inveighs in his room against the unappreciative Otises. They have not yet seen his most famous performances. When they do, they will beg for death! Only little Virginia, who is pretty and gentle and has never insulted him, will be spared. Death and madness to the rest!

Scene 9

Midnight in the corridor as before. Strangled gurgles. Enter the ghost with a rolling gibbet from which he contrives to hang. The twins jump out behind him wearing sheets, and yell "boo!" He screams and flees, dragging the gibbet, and once more topples down the stairs.

Scene 10

Next night. Enter the ghost in rags with a bell. He slouches toward the twins' room shouting, "Unclean, unclean!" and ringing a bell. One twin jumps out and hits him in the face with a huge cream pie. He falls back over the other, who is on all fours behind him. He shambles away howling, and again tumbles down the stairs, as they break up and hug each other.

Scene 11

Next night. Enter the ghost, this time as a hooded headsman with a huge axe. The twins' bedroom door is slightly open. He bursts through with axe uplifted, is drenched by a bucket of water falling from above, and flees again, once more tumbling down the stairs, as the twins screech with laughter.

Scene 12

The ghost sits morosely in his room. He is wrapped in a blanket, with a hot water bottle on his head, his arm in a sling, and his feet in a basin of steaming water. Disgrace! He has been hooted and hectored off the stage! Let the Otises do without him! Let them sleep like lumps! Let them hang! He quits!

Scene 13

The Otises are at breakfast. There has been no sign of the ghost for a week. The twins miss him. Virginia commiserates. Their parents discuss the clambake planned for the next day.

Scene 14

The Otises and their guests, including Canterville and Cheshire, now 18, are seen at the clambake. Projections show badminton, archery, croquet, and riding. Cheshire has asked for Virginia's hand. Otis has declined; they are both too young. That aside, if both become what he believes they will, in a few years, he could imagine no finer match. Mrs. Otis agrees. Meanwhile Virginia has torn her riding habit at one of the jumps, and has gone back to the house to have it mended.

Scene 15

Viriginia has lost her way in the house, and has entered the ghost's room by accident. He is looking out the window. For eight days now, he says, he has kept his silence and his distance. He almost misses the twins, but they have abused him terribly. "They have, Sir Simon," she agrees, "but you should not pretend innocence. Lord Canterville told us that you murdered your brother-in-law." The ghost, now looking at her, admits that "I am guilty as sentenced. He had tried to steal the jewels I had given his sister at our tenth anniversary, and taunted me when I caught him. But I should never have done it. She was the one pure soul in a wicked family, and my deed made me as wicked." Now he can sleep only in the Garden of Death, but death is forbidden for him. If a pure soul intercedes for him, perhaps the Angel of Death will have mercy on him, and he can sleep at last. Could she help? Virginia promises. An opening appears in a tapestry at the back of the room. Voices from the tapestry warn her as she and the ghost walk through.

Scene 16

Late afternoon at the clambake site. All guests are gone except Canterville and Cheshire. Virginia is missing. Perhaps she had been taken by gypsies whom Otis had let camp in the park, and who had now gone to Bexley. Otis will ride to see. Canterville and Cheshire volunteer to join.

Scene 17

The three are at Bexley that night. She isn't there. They will return to Canterville Chase and hope for the best.

Scene 18

Otis, Mrs. Otis, the twins, Canterville and Cheshire are finishing a late supper in the dining room in silence. Otis says that they must try to sleep. "We trust in a kind Providence, and whatever we can do to help it in the morning." The clock strikes one. Virginia appears with a box of jewels. She tells them that the ghost has died, after giving her the jewels, and that they must come to see him. She leads them to the ghost's room. His skeleton lies on the floor. The twins say, "We love you, Sir Simon." Mrs. Otis, looking through the windows in the moonlight, remarks that an almond tree which had withered on the day Sir Simon murdered his brother-in-law, three centuries before, is in full blossom. Virginia says, "God has forgiven him."

Scene 19

Morning, a few days later, in the library. Otis presses Canterville to take back the jewels Sir Simon had given Virginia. "We yankees have no need of them, and in this case no right to them. They would have passed in law to his heirs three centuries ago, and eventually to you." Canterville will hear none of it. "My dear sir, your charming daughter rendered Sir Simon a very important service through her marvelous courage and pluck. The jewels are clearly hers, and Egad, I believe that if I were heartless enough to take them from her, the wicked old fellow would be out of his grave in a fortnight, leading me the devil of a life. Trust your daughter, and Sir Simon's judgment, to put his gift to best use." He claps Otis on the arm good-naturedly as they exit.

Scene 20

Sir Simon's gravesite, autumn afternoon, five years later. Cheshire and Virginia, now married and expecting, are present with Mr. and Mrs. Otis and the twins and Canterville. The twins, now inches taller, are played by other performers. Virginia puts an almond bough on the grave. All leave but Virginia and Cheshire. They sing the love duet "Stay with me, beautiful, in my calling." Cheshire asks what had she seen on her journey with the ghost. She has promised to keep that secret, even from him. "But you will tell our children one day, won't you? Won't you?"

THE CANTERVILLE GHOST
Opera in One Act

Libretto
By Gordon Getty
2012

Adapted from Oscar Wilde

Cast of Characters in Order of Appearance

FIRST BOY, great-grandson of the Otises
Cecil, Duke of CHESHIRE,[129] neighbor of the Canterville Chase and Virginia's future husband
SECOND BOY, great-grandson of the Otises
VIRGINIA, daughter of the Otises
Lord CANTERVILLE, previous owner of Canterville Chase
FIRST TWIN
SECOND TWIN } sons of the Otises
Hiram OTIS
MRS. OTIS } new owners of Canterville Chase
GHOST (Sir Simon), ghost who haunts Canterville Chase
FIRST VOICE/SECOND VOICE (spirits)

NOTE: *Text with a solid line in the left margin indicates original source material. Text with a dot in the left margin indicates adapted source material.*

Scene 1

Sir Simon's gravesite, afternoon, about 1960. Virginia, Cheshire and their descendants of all ages, as many as practical. Two baby carriages.

FIRST BOY
(*To Cheshire*) Great Grandpapa, is there really a ghost here?

---

[129] Pronounced "CHESH-er"

CHESHIRE
(*Age 88*) I have never seen the ghost, so you will have to ask Great Grandmama. On a day as beautiful as this, she led a troubled soul to rest. He was not quite family, as we are, but an old guest in her house. How she did so is a secret between them. It is secret even from me. His name was Sir Simon de Canterville. Ever since, we have come here to bid him safe journey, old and young together, some each year for the first time, and some perhaps for the last. Our trek will not be as long as his.

SECOND BOY
(*To Virginia*) Great Grandmama, is it really true?

VIRGINIA
(*Age 85*) It is true. Do you know the poem on the stained glass window at Canterville Chase?

BOTH BOYS
We do, Great Grandmama.

VIRGINIA
Remember the line "When the barren almond bears"? There stands the almond, and there lies the bough from it that you and I just put on the grave. We have put one there each year. The tree was old in Queen Elizabeth's time, and had long been withered when we bought the Chase. No one remembers any almond to have bloomed so many years, or at all after once barren. The poem told the truth. That is why we inscribed it on his gravestone.

CHESHIRE
You may all read it. It runs (*From memory*)
> "When a golden girl can win
> Prayer from out the lips of sin,
> When the barren almond bears,
> And a little child give away its tears,
> Then shall all the house be still
> And peace come to Canterville."

VIRGINIA
So it happened, little children, seventy years ago.

Scene 2

Library at Canterville Chase, night, about 1890. Large windows at the back, a suit of armor between. Door at one side. Staff except Mrs. Umney lined up facing audience near the door. Mrs. Umney opens it. Enter Canterville, Otis, Mrs. Otis, Virginia (age 15), and Twins (age 12). Mrs. Umney joins the line.

CANTERVILLE
My dear Otises, you have met Mrs. Umney, Barbara, Richard and Mellows. (*They bow or curtsy.*) I trust they will serve you well. (*At a sign, the staff leaves.*) I also hope you will have better luck with Canterville Chase than I and my ancestors did. The ghost is real enough. He has worked his mischief for these three centuries. I fear your beautiful family may be treated no better. It is not too late to withdraw from the purchase now. Sir Simon has brought us Cantervilles in quite enough disrepute without my failure to warn.

FIRST TWIN
(*Delighted*) A ghost!

SECOND TWIN
(*Delighted*) A real ghost! I'll spot him first!

FIRST TWIN
No, I will! (*Both giggle.*)

VIRGINIA
Poor lonely ghost! Poor Sir Simon, alone in the cold!

OTIS
My Lord, I will take the furniture and the ghost at a valuation. I come from a modern country, where we have everything money can buy; and with all our spry young fellows painting the Old World red, and carrying off your best actresses and prima donnas, I reckon that if there were such a thing as a ghost in the whole of Europe, we'd have it at home in a very short time in one of our public museums, or on the road as a show.

CANTERVILLE[130]
Then let us hope Sir Simon accepts the overtures of your enterprising impresarios. If not, as I fear, Richard can ride the seven miles to the train station at Ascot for anything needed. I will do what I can if asked. I gather young Cheshire is in your corner too, and I would value his help in a pinch.

VIRGINIA
O, Father, do!

TWINS
(*Looking at the armor*) Is that the ghost's armor?

CANTERVILLE
It is indeed.

MRS. OTIS
Hiram,[131] what is this mark on it?

CANTERVILLE
If I may answer, it is the blood of Sir Simon's brother-in-law, murdered by him on this spot in 1585. Sir Simon survived nine years, and disappeared suddenly. No trace of him has ever been found. It seems that the victim fell against the armor, and the stain cannot be removed.

FIRST TWIN
A bloodstain!

SECOND TWIN
All the better!

BOTH TWINS
Let's hunt the ghost!

---

[130] This first sentence quotes Wilde.
[131] Pronounced "HY-rum"

OTIS
That is all nonsense! Pinkerton's Champion Stain Remover and Paragon Detergent will clean it up in no time! (*He produces some, and cleans briskly while we hear "Yankee Doodle." The stain disappears.*) I knew Pinkerton's would do it! (*Lightning visible through both windows, loud thunder after half a second. Rain pounds the windows.*) What a monstrous climate! I guess the old country is so overpopulated that they have not enough decent weather for everybody. I have always been of the opinion that emigration is the only thing for England. (*Now we hear "Rule, Brittania." The suit of armor salutes, British style, palm out, at the closing tonic. It squeaks slightly in doing so, and returns to normal just before all look back.*)

CANTERVILLE
(*Smiling*) Well, I shall emigrate home. Good night, good Otises. Remember to call on me in any need, and remember that I warned you.

Scene 3

Library, morning, empty. Sun shining through the windows.

TWINS
(*From outside the door*) Daddy! Hurry! Bring the key!

OTIS
(*From upstairs*) We're coming down now! (*Running footsteps.*)

TWINS
Virginia! Hurry!

Key is heard in the lock. Door opens inward. All enter, twins first. They rush to the suit of armor.

SECOND TWIN
It's here again!

FIRST TWIN
As big as ever!

VIRGINIA
(*Right after them*) Daddy, Mommy, it's the bloodstain again! That's three times in a row!

OTIS
(*Pensively*) And twice with the door locked overnight after I cleaned it away.

MRS. OTIS
Hiram, dear, it might be the ghost after all.

FIRST TWIN
It is!

SECOND TWIN
For sure!

BOTH TWINS
Let's find him! We'll pull his sheet!

VIRGINIA
It must be. Poor cold ghost.

MRS. OTIS
Hiram, perhaps we were a little hasty. Do you think I should join the Psychical Society? It would do no harm.

OTIS[132]
Perhaps we were. Live and learn. If there is a ghost after all, it's only fair that he should pay us rent. (*The suit of armor stiffens in alarm.*) I will draft a letter to the firm of Myers and Podmore on the matter, as well as an article on the Permanence of Sanguinous Stains when Connected with Crime. Meanwhile, we will clean it as fast as the ghost restores it, if the Pinkerton supply holds up, and at least be rid of it in between. We Yankees can be stubborn too. (*He motions them toward the door, and opens it. Through the doorway*) Mrs. Umney, let us have some breakfast!

---

[132] In Wilde, Myers and Podmore are the publishers to which Otis plans to send the article. I turn them into a law firm.

Scene 4

A corridor upstairs, midnight. Clanking of chains. Ghost enters dragging chains and moaning, lurches slowly toward the Otis bedroom. He arrives. Door opens from inside. Otis emerges.

OTIS
(*Composed, to Ghost*) My dear sir, I really must insist on your oiling those chains, and have brought you for that purpose a small supply of the Tammany Rising Sun Lubricator. (*Holds it up.*) It is said to be completely efficacious upon one application, and there are several testimonials to that effect upon the wrapper from some of our most eminent native divines.

Otis hands it to him and gently closes the door. Ghost is thunderstruck. Then he dashes the bottle on the floor, roaring indignation, and lurches back the way he came. Twins, emerging from a door, whiz pillows past his head. He reverses direction, flees, and tumbles down the stairs.

Scene 5

Ghost's room, immediately after. A door on one side wall, a window on the other. Back wall is covered by a large tapestry with a hunting scene. Ghost enters from the door in a rage, and begins throwing his chains on a ring hanging near it.

GHOST (Sir Simon)[133]
Rising Sun Lubricator! Pillows! Never, in a career of three hundred years, have I been so grossly insulted! What of my achievements? I am an artist! Think of the wicked Lord Lackton choking in his dressing room with the knave of diamonds half-way down his throat, and confessing, just before he died, that he had cheated Charles James Fox of 50,000 pounds at Crockford's by means of that very card, and that I had made him swallow it. An artist! Think of my triumph as "Red Reuben, or The Strangled Babe"! My debut as "Gaunt Gibeon, the Blood-Sucker of Bexley Moor"! All the world was in awe! To see me was to take one's life, or die of fright, or babble in asylums! And now some wretched modern Americans offer me the Rising Sun Lubricator, and throw pillows at my head! An artist! It is not to be borne! An artist gives such

---

[133] The lines about Lord Lackton, Lord Raker's wig and Gaugin are Wilde's.

an audience a performance worthy of himself, not of their thick perceptions. They have not heard my maniacal laugh, that turned Lord Raker's wig grey in a single night! They will! They will! (*Illustrates the laugh.*)

Scene 6

Morning. Dining room on one side of the stage, library with the suit of armor on the other, and a wall between. Otises, Virginia and twins are eating breakfast in the dining room. All but Otis mime conversation. Otis' attention is divided among this, a newspaper by his place and a cup of coffee in his hand. Staff waiting. Otis puts down the coffee, turns the page, picks up the coffee again, takes a sip. Meanwhile the suit of armor (Ghost) tippy-toes delicately across the library, like Sylvester sneaking up on Tweetie Pie, to the door in the wall between. He cracks it open slightly and cups his hand to his ear.

OTIS
I confess disappointment that my gift to the ghost has not been accepted. I have no wish to do him any personal injury, and I must say that considering the length of time that he has been in the house, I don't think it is at all polite to throw pillows at him. (*Twins whoop with laughter.*) Upon the other hand, if he really declines to use the Rising Sun Lubricator, we will have to take his chains from him. It would be quite impossible to sleep with such a noise going on outside the bedrooms. This would be the minimum step. The firm of Myers and Podmore assure me that eviction proceedings on the grounds of nuisance, let alone evasion of rent, would otherwise be quite in order. (*Resumes reading as Ghost mimes indignation.*)

MRS. OTIS[134]
But, Hiram, would that be fair? (*Otis looks up.*) Some consideration should be given an artist. His nightly movements are performances of a sort, and he has not actually done us harm. His manner of restoring the bloodstains each morning suggests that he has taken an interest in Paul Gaugin. (*She pronounces it Gow-GEEN.*)

---

[134] Ibid.

GHOST
Gaugin! (*Pronounced correctly in a stage whisper. He then closes the door silently, and tippy-toes back to his stand.*)

MRS. OTIS
... Gaugin (*Correctly this time*), and the impressionists. Different colors every day! (*Now she does a doubletake, staring at the door, as the twins continue.*)

TWINS
The ghost is colorblind! Let's bet on what he will pick next! (*Giggles.*)

VIRGINIA
That isn't funny at all!

OTIS
Dears, dears! We will take his chains if he does not use the oil, and that is quite enough. The house has room for all of us if he leaves us in peace. It is the oil or the chains. Artists are artists, but my guests must follow minimum rules.

MRS. OTIS
My dear, you are quite right, as always. (*To Barbara as Otis resumes reading*) Barbara, could we have more toast? (*Barbara hurries toward the kitchen.*)

Scene 7

Midnight in the upstairs corridor again. Ghost enters. No chains, but he wears the suit of armor from the library. The bloodstain is emerald green. Moaning and groaning. He reaches the Otis' bedroom door as before, clears his throat, and lets loose the maniacal laugh again. The door opens as he finishes. Mrs. Otis appears.

MRS. OTIS
I fear you are far from well, and have brought you a bottle of Dr. Dobell's Tincture. If it is indigestion, you will find it a most excellent remedy. Artists such as yourself are given to delicate constitutions, and owe the public due attention to their health.

She closes the door gently as had Otis. Ghost dashes the tincture as he had the lubricator, with howls of indignation. Twins ambush him with pea-shooters. Again he flees, and tumbles down the stairs, as they shriek with laughter.

Scene 8

Ghost's room, immediately after. Ghost is throwing off the armor.

GHOST
Insupportable! To be lectured on professionalism! On hygiene! On my duty to the audience! After being called an imitator of Gauguin! Performances of a sort! Of a sort! Do they think I don't listen? What is an artist to an audience of oysters? A public of poultry and potatoes! A claque of cucumbers! All euphemisms for Americans. They are what Americans hope to become if they are good. Death to all! Death and Thunder! Murder will walk abroad with silent feet. The twins first! They have not seen my "Dumb Daniel, or the Suicide's Skeleton"! None who have seen it are alive and sane. And the Otises! They will get my "Martin the Maniac or the Masked Mystery"! They will beg for death! Only little Virginia, who has never insulted me, and is pretty and gentle, will be spared. A few hollow groans from the wardrobe should be enough. No ghost could honorably do less. Death and madness to the rest!

Scene 9

Next night. Upstairs, as before. Strangled gurgles. Ghost enters with a rolling gibbet from which he contrives to hang. The twins jump out in sheets, yelling, "Boo!" He screams and flees, dragging the gibbet, and again tumbles with it down the stairs.

Scene 10

Next night. Enter Ghost in rags with a bell. He slouches toward the twins' room shouting, "Unclean, unclean!" and ringing the bell. One twin jumps out and hits him in the face with a huge cream pie. He falls back over the other who is on all fours behind him. He scrambles away howling, and again tumbles down the stairs, as they break up and hug each other, jumping up and down.

Scene 11

Next night. Enter Ghost, this time as a hooded headsman with a huge axe. The twins' bedroom door is slightly open. He bursts through with axe uplifted, is drenched by a bucket of water falling from above, and flees again, once more tumbling down the stairs, as the twins screech with laughter.

Scene 12

Ghost's room. Ghost sits wrapped in a blanket, a hot water bottle on his head, his arm in a sling, his feet in a steaming basin of water. He is morose.

GHOST
Fiasco! Disgrace! (*Sneezing*) A-choo! Hooted and hectored off the stage! Enough! No more! A-choo! Let them sleep like lumps! Let them do without me! Let them do without the bloodstain! Let them hang! I withdraw! I cancel! I abrogate! I quit! A-choo!

Scene 13

Dining room alone, a week later, without the library visible at one side. Otises, Virginia and the twins are at breakfast. Again a newspaper by Otis' place. Staff serving.

OTIS
(*To all the family as they eat*) Again no bloodstain on the armor. It has been a week since the last.

MRS. OTIS
And no noises or visits in the night. Might Sir Simon have gone?

VIRGINIA
Mommy, where? This is his home.

FIRST TWIN
We miss him.

SECOND TWIN
We need Sir Simon!

OTIS
He may not have gone. I am missing a jar of the Rising Sun Lubricator.

MRS. OTIS
And I a bottle of Dr. Dobell's Tincture.

OTIS
And he put the armor back on its stand in the library, although the servants had to shine away the scratches and scuff marks. Possibly he has mended his manners.

MRS. OTIS
An artist would need some pause for sabbatical or vacation.

OTIS
Then let us hope it holds for tomorrow's clambake. All our friends and neighbors have accepted. I almost miss Sir Simon, to tell the truth, but we will have enough to manage without him.

MRS. OTIS
Indeed we will. I do so look forward to seeing Lord Canterville again, and young Duke Cecil[135] of Cheshire. And Cecil may also interest someone else here.

VIRGINIA
Mommy, stop!

TWINS
Sir Simon, come back! We promise to be afraid!

FIRST TWIN
(*Sotto voce*) But not too much! (*Giggles.*)

---

[135] Pronounced "SEH-suhl"

Scene 14

Clambake. Afternoon, outside. House in background. Archery, badminton, riding, croquet. Canterville, Cheshire (age 18), Otises, Virginia, Twins, servants, guests.

CANTERVILLE
(*To Otises*) I hear the ghost has packed his bags. Congratulations all round, and well done! He had done dreadful things in the Chase, and I would not have wanted any of them to have happened to you.

OTIS
My lord, we are not so sure. A pause at least. We had grown accustomed to the old sinner, but welcome the extra sleep.

CANTERVILLE
Then let us hope for the best. Remember to count on me, and on young Cheshire, if trouble comes back. (*Presses his hand. To a guest*) Lady Harriet! (*Moves off.*)

MRS. OTIS
(*Joining Otis*) Dear Hiram! I'm happy to see that young Cheshire came by a few minutes ago. Did he ask for Virginia's hand again?

OTIS
He did, and got the same answer. They are both too young. And we Americans, for ourselves, are happiest with no titles other than Mr. and Mrs. I told him that that aside, if both become what I believe they will in a few years, I could imagine no finer match.

MRS. OTIS
My thoughts exactly. Have they been riding together?

OTIS
They have, and both took the third hedge cleanly. She just tore her habit on the fourth and is going inside to get Barbara to mend it.

MRS. OTIS
There she is at the service door now. Barbara will be making tea. I'll go help her. (*Starts off.*)

Scene 15

Ghost's room, immediately after. Ghost sits looking out gloomily through the window.

VIRGINIA
(*Offstage*) Barbara! Barbara! Does anyone hear me? Barbara! (*Enters carrying torn riding habit.*) Sir Simon! (*She approaches softly as he continues looking through the window. To Ghost*) I am so sorry for you, but my brothers are going back to Eton soon, and if you behave yourself, no one will annoy you.

GHOST
(*Still looking out*) Behaving oneself does not come easily to a ghost. For eight days now, I have oiled my chains, and taken my tincture, and kept my silence. I shall almost miss the twins, but they have abused me terribly. Let them be the terror of Eton, and not of old residents at Canterville.

VIRGINIA
They have, Sir Simon, but you should not pretend innocence. Lord Canterville told us that you murdered your brother-in-law.

GHOST
(*Now looking at her*) I am justly sentenced. He tried to steal the jewels I had given his sister at our tenth anniversary, and taunted me when I caught him. But I should never have done it. She was the one pure soul in a wicked family, and my deed made me as wicked. They came nine years later, and captured me here in this room. There are the chains by which they bound me to the wall, and there are the bowls of food and water just out of my reach. They wanted her jewels, but never got them. I perished where they bound me.

VIRGINIA
Starve you to death? Oh, Mister Ghost, I mean Sir Simon, are you hungry? I have a sandwich here in my pack. (*Takes it out.*) Would you like it?

GHOST
No, thank you, I never eat anything now; but it is very kind of you, all the same, and you are much nicer than the rest of your horrid, rude, vulgar, dishonest family.

VIRGINIA

Stop! (*Stamps her foot.*) It is you who are rude and horrid and vulgar, and as for dishonesty, you know you stole the paints out of my box (*Projections show him doing these things.*) to try to furbish up that ridiculous bloodstain on the armor. First you took all my reds, including the vermillion, and I couldn't do any more sunsets. Then you took the emerald green and the chrome yellow, and finally I had nothing left but indigo and Chinese white, and could only do moonlight scenes, which are always depressing to look at, and not at all easy to paint. I never told on you, though I was very much annoyed, and it was most ridiculous, the whole thing; for who ever heard of emerald green blood?

GHOST

(*Rather meekly*) Well, there you have me. It seems I am not much of a ghost. I could frighten as well as the next, until your family bought the Chase, but I could never stand the sight of blood. Can you imagine? In a ghost? I could not look at my brother-in-law's, while putting on the armor, for three centuries until your father cleaned it away. My duty then was to restore it, and I could find no other way. (*Shrugging, palms forward*) What good is a ghost who could never do worse than frighten, and now not even that?

VIRGINIA

You could come to America. I know lots of people there who would pay ten thousand dollars just to have a grandfather, (*Wide-eyed, playing it straight*) and much more than that to have a family ghost.

GHOST

(*Petulantly*) I don't think I should like America.

VIRGINIA

(*Angered*) I suppose because we have no ruins and no curiosities!

GHOST

(*Angered in return*) No ruins! No curiosities! You have your navy and your manners.

VIRGINIA

(*Spinning toward the door*) Good evening! I will go and ask Papa to get the twins an extra week's holiday! (*Starts off.*)

GHOST
(*Catching her hand, rueful*) Please don't go, Miss Virginia. I am so lonely and so unhappy, and I really don't know what to do. I want to go to sleep and I cannot. For three hundred years, I have not slept, and I am so tired.

VIRGINIA
(*Kneeling by his side*) Poor, poor ghost! Have you no place where you can sleep?

GHOST
Far away beyond the pine woods, there is a little garden. There the grass grows long and deep, there are the great white stars of the hemlock flower, there the nightingale sings all night long. All night long he sings, and the cold, crystal moon looks down, and the yew-tree spreads out its giant arms over the sleepers.

VIRGINIA
(*Her face in her hands*) You mean the Garden of Death.

GHOST
Yes. Death must be so beautiful. To lie in the soft, brown earth, and listen to silence. To forget time, to forgive life, to be at peace. You can help me. You can open for me the portals of Death's house, for Love is always with you, and Love is stronger than Death is. (*Virginia shudders.*) Have you ever read the old prophecy on the library window?

VIRGINIA
(*Looking up*) Oh, often! It is painted in curious black letters, and it is difficult to read. It goes:
"When a golden girl can win
Prayer from out the lips of sin,
When the barren almond bears,
And a little child give away its tears,
Then shall all the house be still
And peace come to Canterville."

But I don't know what it means.

GHOST[136]
You can see the tree through this window, on the hill past the meadow. (*Virginia looks.*) It withered on the day I murdered my brother-in-law. The words mean that you must weep with me for my sins, because I have no tears, and pray with me for my soul, because I have no faith, and then, if you have always been sweet, and good, and gentle, the Angel of Death will have mercy on me. You will see fearful shapes in darkness, and wicked voices will whisper in your ear, but they will not harm you, for against the purity of a little child the powers of Hell cannot prevail.

VIRGINIA
(*Rising*) I am not afraid, and I will ask the Angel to have mercy on you. (*Ghost rises, kisses her hand, leads her toward the tapestry.*)

FIRST VOICE
(*From the tapestry*) Go back, little Virginia, go back!

SECOND VOICE
(*From the tapestry*) Beware! We may never see you again!

At a sign from Ghost, a space opens in the tapestry to reveal a cavern.

GHOST
Quick, quick, or it will be too late! (*They pass through as the wall closes behind.*)

Scene 16

Late afternoon, clambake site with house in background as before, guests gone.

MRS. OTIS
(*From an upstairs window*) Hiram, she is nowhere in the house. No one has seen her.

OTIS
(*Entering stage right*) She is not on the property. Canterville and Cheshire have stayed to help. I will wire the police.

---

[136] All but the first two sentences quote Wilde.

FIRST TWIN
(*From another upstairs window*) She isn't anywhere!

SECOND TWIN
We can't find her!

CANTERVILLE
(*Entering stage left with Cheshire*) She is nowhere. The station master at Ascot has telegraphed up and down the line.

OTIS
It may be the gypsies I let camp in the park. I will ride to see.

CANTERVILLE
Richard has just come back from there. The gypsies left earlier in a rush.

OTIS
They may have gone back to Bexley. I will look for them there.

CANTERVILLE
Let me help.

CHESHIRE[137]
And me.

OTIS
Willingly, good Canterville and Cecil. But there must not be a scuffle. We have no reason yet to suspect them. Richard will saddle the horses. I will wire the police now.

Scene 17

That night, Bexley Moor. Canterville and Cheshire emerge from gypsy camp in background as Otis enters to meet them.

---

[137] Wilde does not include Cheshire in scenes XVI through XVIII.

CANTERVILLE
She isn't here. They had heard of our trouble and want to help. They had mistaken the date of Chorton Fair and went off this morning in a hurry not to miss it.

OTIS
Richard overtook us just now and said that Mellows and his men have dragged the carp pond. There is no trace, thank heaven.

CHESHIRE
Thank heaven! We must telegraph Scotland Yard in the morning.

OTIS
And hope for the best. There is nothing more to do until then. Back to Canterville Chase, where we will take supper and what rest we can.

CHESHIRE
I cannot sleep.

Scene 18

Canterville Chase, dining room, same night. Otis, Mrs. Otis, Twins, Canterville, Cheshire at table. Staff serving supper. All silent.

OTIS
Thank you, Mrs. Umney. You may all go to bed now, and sleep if you can. (*Servants leave. To the rest*) As each of us finishes, we must do the same. We trust in a kind Providence, and whatever we can do to help it in the morning.

All begin to rise. The clock strikes one. A flash of light. Virginia appears in the alcove with a small box of jewels. She descends. All rush to her.

MRS. OTIS
(*Flustered, out of breath*) Good heavens, child! Where have you been? We have been riding all over the country looking for you, and your mother has been frightened to death. You must never play these practical jokes any more.

TWINS
(*Gleefully*) Except on the ghost! Except on the ghost!

MRS. OTIS
My own darling, thank God you are found; you must never leave my side again.

VIRGINIA
Papa, I have been with the ghost. He is dead, and you must come and see him. He had been very wicked, but he was really sorry for all that he had done, and he gave me this box of beautiful jewels before he died. (*She leads them all to the Ghost's room. His skeleton lies in the chains. Virginia kneels and prays silently.*)

Illustration from *The Canterville Ghost* • Evgenija Chistotina

TWINS
(*To the skeleton*) We love you, Sir Simon.

MRS. OTIS
(*Seeing something through the window*) Hiram, look! The old withered almond tree has blossomed. It is clear in the moonlight. I have never seen such a thing. (*All but Virginia rush to see.*)

VIRGINIA
God has forgiven him. (*Cheshire squeezes her hand.*)

Scene 19

Morning, a few days later. Library. Otis and Canterville.

CANTERVILLE
My good Otis, thank you for putting me up again for the funeral of Sir Simon yesterday, and for attending yourself with your family and staff. It had been delayed three centuries, and mourners who knew him would otherwise have been scarce.

OTIS
My lord, we were honored. He was an unruly guest, but one with grievances, and he was generous in the end. It is of that that I must speak to you. The jewels are your rightful property. I press you to take them. They would have passed in law to his heirs three centuries past, and so eventually to you. We Yankees have no need of them, and in this case, no right to them. Virginia entreats you only to let her keep the box, which seems to be of no value, as a memento of your unhappy ancestor.

CANTERVILLE[138]
My dear sir, your charming daughter rendered Sir Simon a very important service through her marvelous courage and pluck. The jewels are clearly hers, and Egad, I believe that if I were heartless enough to take them from her, the wicked old fellow would be out of his grave in a fortnight, leading me the devil of a life. Besides, you forget, Mr. Otis, that you took the furniture

---

[138] All but the last sentence here quotes Wilde.

and the ghost at a valuation, and own whatever comes of them. Trust your daughter, and Sir Simon's judgment, to put his gift to best use.

OTIS
But my lord, my lord … (*Canterville claps him on the arm good-naturedly as they exit.*)

Scene 20

Gravesite, autumn afternoon, five years later. Otis, Mrs. Otis, Virginia, Twins, Cheshire, Canterville, baby carriages. Cheshire and Virginia now married. Twins, inches taller than before, are mimed by actors. Virginia puts an almond bough on Sir Simon's grave.

ALL
"Then shall all the house be still
And peace come to Canterville."

CHESHIRE
And to Sir Simon.

ALL
Amen.

OTIS
At any rate, the almond is still bearing.

CANTERVILLE
And the happy couple. Dear Otises, you are blessed.

MRS. OTIS
We are, and in friendship no less, dear Lord Canterville.

OTIS
In family and friendship too. Now let's all go in for tea.

CHESHIRE
Virginia and I will be there in a bit. (*Exeunt all but Cheshire and Virginia.*)

Stay with me, beautiful, in my calling,
Autumn is here and the leaves are falling,
One by one,
Stay with me, beauty, until the night is done.

VIRGINIA
Take me wherever the summer goes,
Carry it back again, rose by rose,
And song by song,
Stay with me, beautiful, all the night along.

BOTH
Stay with me, beautiful, in my keeping;
Autumn is here and the woods are sleeping,
Rose and song,
Stay with me, beautiful, all the night along.

CHESHIRE
(*Takes both her hands, looks in her eyes.*) Virginia, a wife should have no secrets from her husband.

VIRGINIA
Dear Cecil, I have no secrets from you.

CHESHIRE[139]
Yes, you have. You have never told me what happened to you on your journey with the ghost.

VIRGINIA
I have never told anyone, Cecil.

CHESHIRE
I know that, but you might tell me.

VIRGINIA
Please don't ask me, Cecil. I cannot tell you. Poor Sir Simon! I owe him a great deal, I really do. He made me see what Life is and what Death signifies, and why Love is stronger than both.

---

[139] "when you were locked up," not "on your journey."

CHESHIRE
Once upon a golden day
A golden girl went far away,
And what she saw, she did not say,
But she said "yes" to me.

VIRGINIA
And when she went, a gallant band
Went hunting for her through the land.
One took her hand, and took her heart,
For all the time to be.

CHESHIRE
For all the time to be.

(*They embrace.*) You can have your secret as long as I have your heart.

VIRGINIA
You have always had that, Cecil.

Take me wherever the summer goes,
Carry it back again, rose by rose,
And song by song,
Stay with me, beautiful, all the night along.

BOTH
Stay with me, beautiful, in my keeping;
Autumn is here and the woods are sleeping,
Rose and song,
Stay with me, beautiful, all the night along.

Stay with me, beautiful, in my calling,
Autumn is here and the leaves are falling,
One by one,
Stay with me, beauty, until the night is done.

CHESHIRE
And you will tell our children someday, won't you? Won't you? (*She looks away shyly. Their eyes meet again. Curtain.*)

GOODBYE, MR. CHIPS

Illustration: © A+E=Balbusso Twins

Goodbye, Mr. Chips (Program Notes)

Hilton's masterpiece is largely a series of vignettes where few characters, Chips and Kathie aside, appear or are mentioned in more than one scene. Opera and the spoken stage tend to work best when we follow a few characters over time. Thus Doctor Merrivale, who is found only in the opening scene of the book, becomes the narrator who guides us through the opera. Likewise Kathie reappears in flashbacks long after her early death in childbirth.

One of the recurring themes in the book is the loss of Chips' old students, one after another, in the Great War. I express this powerful idea by making sure that all three students whom we meet by name before the war die in it, and are seen again in ghostly presence as Chips reports their loss to the student body in chapel, and once more in his deathbed delirium.

Chips' antagonist is the overbearing new headmaster Ralston, who sees Chips' ways as slack and old-fashioned, and demands that Chips retire. Ralston gets his comeuppance when the school backs Chips. He moves on, and does not reappear in the novel. I adapt one of Hilton's short stories about Chips to bring Ralston back at the end. In that story, an old student faces twelve years in prison for grand larceny, worries that the scandal will ruin the chances of his son's admission to Brookfield, and asks and receives Chips' promise to help. I make the son a grandson, and turn the old student into Ralston.

These retouches to expand the roles of Merrivale, Kathie, the three students and Ralston allow the audience to see familiar faces and hear familiar voices from scene to scene. That somehow seemed right to me, and offered the practical advantages of role consolidation without much changing of Hilton's beautiful design.

One problem in staging the opera is Chips' quick changes in age from 85 to 48, and then back again, in the scenes of Kathie's first appearance in Act I, and her last near the end of Act 2. One nice solution is for an actor to mime the few lines of the 48-year-old Chips while the real Chips sings them, just as they do in the scene of Chips' vigil, in Act 2, where Chips prays for the rescue of Grayson's father.

Another issue in staging concerns the Linford scene near the end of Act 2. Kathie, on her deathbed, had promised Chips, "I will knock on your door, and take your hand, and help you down the mountain one more time." My idea, and Hilton's too, I think, is that Kathie is somehow keeping her word through Linford. I make this point clear to the audience by requiring the soprano who sings Kathie to sing Linford also. It is also possible for her to act the part herself, or for a child actor to mime it while she is seen or projected singing from behind or outside.

Goodbye, Mr. Chips (Synopsis)

Act I

We hear children singing "Alma Mater," a school song in Latin. Merrivale tells how Chips—"Mister Chipping" or "sir" by the students to his face—became a legend over 48 years of teaching Latin at Brookfield, an English boarding school for boys. We first see Chips, now 85 and retired, with Merrivale, his doctor, in Chips' drawing room across the street from Brookfield. It is 1933. Chips tells Merrivale how he had met Kathie, a girl with golden hair, on vacation in the Lake District in 1896. They had married within weeks. We see them on the eve of their wedding, and then celebrating in Brookfield as they expect their first child. He buys baby clothes, a rattle, a music box. But she dies in childbirth, and the baby is stillborn. The doctors had warned of complications. We see her farewell to Chips at the hospital (Kathie's aria). Her last words to him are: "I will save a place for you, if I am sent the right way, and keep an eye on you, if their telescopes are strong enough, and put in a word for you, if I can find the right ear, because I love you forever and ever and ever. Goodbye, Mr. Chips."

Merrivale tells us the rest. Chips gradually shows the gentle whimsies half-expected in senior schoolmasters. Kathie has become a part of him. He wears the same old gown for years because Kathie had stitched it once. He slips more humor into his lectures to help the boys understand and remember, just as Kathie had thought he should. We see his kindly reaction when one student, Faulkner, plays a prank on him. We see him reprimand another, West, for fighting a neighbor boy. The normal penalty is expulsion. Chips puts the fear of God into West, but lets him off with probation and 200 lines. Alone, Chips says, "The head would rusticate him if he knew. But West has good stuff in him. Kathie, I think that this is what you would have done."

Headmaster Meldrum dies. Chips becomes acting head, and delivers the eulogy. The new headmaster, Ralston, a stern authoritarian, faults Chips for his tattered gown and old-fashioned Latin pronunciation. He demands that Chips retire. Chips is angered but amused as to both criticisms, and declines with wit and grace. "I don't intend to retire," he says, closing the door politely, "and you can do what you like about it." The scene is overheard. The whole school learns of it. All back Chips. The chairman of the board of governors,

Sir John Rivers, tells him, "You can stay here until you're a hundred, if you feel like it. Indeed, it's our hope that you will."

Act 2

Ralston has moved on. The young new head, Chatteris, is a decent sort who lets Chips carry on as before. We see Chips hosting the boys the night before they leave for Christmas holidays. Later he consoles one of them, Grayson, when his father was thought lost on the Titanic. Alone, Chips kneels and prays: "Kathie, beautiful Kathie, if you can find the right ear, please put in a word for Grayson's father." Grayson soon runs in. He is overjoyed. His father has been found safe.

Chips retires at 65, and speaks at a dinner in his honor. He tells anecdotes, some humorous and some touching, of his long teaching career. He adds, "But chiefly, I remember all your faces. I have thousands of faces in my mind, the faces of boys. If you come and see me in years to come, and I hope you will, I shall try to place those older faces of yours, but it's just possible I shan't be able to, and you will say, 'the old boy doesn't remember me.' But I *do* remember you, as you are *now*. That's the point. In my mind, you never grow up at all."

Chatteris leaves to serve in World War I. Chips is invited back to fill in once more as acting head. We see him, as such, reading the list of alumni who have died that week. We see West, Faulkner and Grayson, still boys, as their names are called. Sirens interrupt him. German airplanes are attacking nearby military bases. The building shakes. Chips resumes as if nothing were amiss, and arranges for one boy, Maynard, to find a quote from Caesar that ends the scene in laughter.

We return to Chips' drawing room in 1933, soon after Merrivale has left. The doorbell rings. It is Ralston. He begs Chips' pardon and advice. He says, "Tomorrow I will be arrested for grand larceny. I will plead guilty, and serve twelve years in prison … There is another choice. There is also the gentleman's way … Is there a God, Mr. Chipping?" Chips answers, "There's one inside." "Yes," Ralston says, "there is." He will serve the twelve years. Now he asks another favor. He has applied to Brookfield on behalf of his grandson, and is worried about the scandal. Chips promises.

Chips is also visited by Linford, a new student. A lady had told him to come. As he leaves, he says, "Goodbye, Mr. Chips!" Chips, alone, says, "Mr. Chips! Just like dear Kathie!" He nods off, and slumps to the floor.

He revives in the hospital bed where Kathie died. Merrivale, Rivers, Chatteris and Maynard, now a member of parliament, stand by. Chips tells Rivers of his promise to Ralston. "Scandals be damned," says Rivers, "the boy will be admitted!" Chips nods off again. Maynard, who had talked to Linford, mentions the visit and the lady. "A lady," muses Merrivale, "with golden hair." "Yes! So he told me. Do you know her, Merrivale?" "Only by description." "Pity," says Rivers, "pity that he never had any children." Students outside are heard singing "Alma Mater." Chips wakens. He says, "I heard you, one of you, say that I never had any children. Oh, but I have, I have! Thousands of 'em, and all boys." He calls their names. Again these include Faulkner, Grayson and West. All answer. "Did you hear my last joke?" he asks. "Did it make you laugh? Kathie, did it make you laugh?" He dies.

GOODBYE, MR. CHIPS
Opera in Two Acts

Libretto
By Gordon Getty
2017

Based on the book *Goodbye, Mr. Chips and other stories*
By James Hilton

Cast of Characters in Order of Appearance

MERRIVALE, Chips' physician
CHIPS, formally Mr. Chipping, a teacher at Brookfield
KATHIE, Chips' wife
FAULKNER
WEST } students at Brookfield
RALSTON, Chips' second headmaster at Brookfield
Sir John RIVERS, Chairman of the Board of Governors at Brookfield
GRAYSON
MAYNARD } students at Brookfield
LINFORD

NOTE: Text with a solid line in the left margin indicates original source material. Text with a dot in the left margin indicates adapted source material.

Act I

While the audience files in, projections show Brookfield in an English countryside. Texts of the Latin chorus and translation are superimposed as the singers begin. After they finish the first line, the word projections remain while the background changes from the winter sky to black-and-white photos, optionally intermixing movie clips, showing Brookfield 1870 – 1933.

CHORUS (unseen)

Alma mater, amnis pratum,	Alma mater, Brookfield,
Custos nostrum es.	You are our guardian.
Cantum nostrum audi, mater,	Hear our song, Mother,
Tibi praebitum.	Offered to you.
Stellae dum lapsaverint	Until the stars fall,
In perpetuum,	Forever,
Recordata eris tu	We will remember you
Nocte dieque.	Night and day.
Usque ad diluculum,	Until the dawn,
Nunc et postea	Now and hereafter,
Elucebis denique,	You will shine forth to the last,
Hic et ubivis.	Here and everywhere.

Scenes of Brookfield now illustrate the narrative of Dr. Merrivale, 35, as he moves unnoticed among them.

MERRIVALE
Chips was the soul of Brookfield. Forty-eight years a teacher there, living the last twenty-two of them here, across the street at Mrs. Wickett's, then a kind of semi-retirement there. He remained the guest of honor at Old Brookfeldian dinners. He was the Court of Appeals in matters of Brookfield history and tradition. He knew all of the students to the end, greeting them all by name as they tipped their caps to him on the street or on the playing fields. I had been calling on him, at the last, every fortnight or so. He seemed as hale as always, that dull November afternoon in '33. He greeted me at the door, asked of my wife and our children, our plans for the winter. All bounce and warmth and spark, the same old Chips. But eighty-five is a ripe old age, and he had caught a chill that wanted watching.

Fade to Chips' drawing room at Mrs. Wickett's. A window shows fog. Merrivale is putting away his stethoscope. Chips is buttoning his shirt.

MERRIVALE
Chips, my good fellow, you're fitter than I am. You'll outlive us all. Stay indoors for a while, even so, and early to bed. You know how to ring me, night or day, if the sniffles act up.

CHIPS
(*Age 85*) So I will, good Merrivale. Nothing wrong with me except anno domini, and that hunts us all down at the last. (*Merrivale chuckles.*) It's tea and soup and blankets for me, just now, and memories. A treasury of them, Merrivale, a treasury. Wonderful memories, all but a few, and sixty-three years of them here. One day, perhaps, when you have time …

MERRIVALE
I have now. I would very much like to hear them.

Chips pours sherry. Projections may illustrate his account as he continues.

CHIPS
Memories, then! I arrived here in 1870, aged twenty-two, first having taught for a year at Medbury.[140] It was old Wetherby's last year as headmaster. He said, "I see you had discipline problems at Medbury. No matter. This is a new start. Our boys and theirs are the kindest in the world, Mr. Chipping, one at a time, but a roomful of them is a lion's den. (*Opens the window. Fog drifts in. "Alma Mater" is heard again.*) They will maul you to shreds unless you crack down from the first." I knew that from Medbury, and took it to heart. (*Both men laugh.*)

CHIPS
My very first class was prep.[141] (*Chips closes the window.*) Talk about a lion's den! There were all five hundred of the good-hearted ruffians in Big Hall, ready to pounce. I walked in, grim as a headsman. (*Acting it out as Merrivale enjoys the performance.*) Somebody dropped a desktop. Evenly, calmly, the headsman, the lion tamer, I asked, "Who did that?" No one spoke. "Then you all have a hundred lines." One boy stood up and owned the deed. "Then you alone have a hundred lines." No problem after that! (*Merrivale laughs as Chips continues.*) The boy is now Viscount Colley. He and I laughed when his son tried the same sort of trick on me, to get the same lesson, and later his grandson as well. (*Merrivale laughs again.*) Sixty-three years! Think of it, Merrivale! The Franco-Prussian war, the Boers, the Kaiser, and now Hoover and Baldwin and the slump. (*Stands to pour again.*) And Kathie. Halfway along, for only a little while, there was Kathie. (*Sits down.*) We met in the

---

[140] Pronounced "MED-b'ry"
[141] Supervised homework at the end of the school day.

summer of '96 in the Lake District. I was climbing Great Gable. A girl on a ledge looked in trouble. A girl with golden hair. I ran to her, hurt my own foot, and she had to help **me** down the mountain. (*Both men laugh. The room fades gradually to projections tracing Chips' narrative.*) She looked in on me every day, riding her bicycle 'round the lake to the inn where I stayed. We were Miss Bridges and Mister Chipping down the mountain, Kathie and Chips the day after, hopelessly in love in two weeks, and married in London a week after that. The night before our wedding, as I dropped her off at her aunt's house in Ealing, I remember that she said something curious …

A house on a street in Ealing in 1896. Chips is opening the door for Kathie. They kiss.

KATHIE
Goodbye, Mister Chips!

CHIPS
Dear Kathie! As if my name were really that! Then we shall be Mr. and Mrs. Chips tomorrow!

KATHIE
Tomorrow and always, and little Chips off the two old blocks!

CHIPS
Off us two old blockheads for always! Mr. and Mrs. and baby Chips for always! (*They kiss again.*)

Chips and Merrivale back in Chips' drawing room in 1933.

CHIPS
She won every heart at Brookfield as easily as mine. She was all sunlight, all surprise, all gifts and all giving. (*Fade to Brookfield concert hall, projections only, as Chips continues. Chips may be seen or unseen as projections change to follow his narrative.*) I remember her playing the cello in a Mozart trio at a school concert, her white[142] arm sweeping the bow against the brown sheen of the instrument. (*Rising*) She was everything young and beautiful, everything new and forever, wise and merry, quick and deep, footsure. She was the spark,

---

[142] "creamy," not "white"

the glow, the pulse and current of my life and all our lives. All loved her, all trusted her, the masters, their wives, the boys, chars, cooks, tradesmen, all, because they knew that she could see with their own eyes. She could see them from inside. She knew which boys, despite all, were worth one more chance. She knew that the boys are our measure and our chronicle and our future. It was she who showed me that we can't really teach them, but must help them teach themselves, since that's the learning that holds and builds and stands up to whatever comes outside. That's the secret. It's the boys, the boys, and whatever mix of patience and wit and guidance and guile and fear of hellfire will trick them into teaching themselves! "Chips, dearest," she said, "you have the gift of making them laugh in just the right places, so that they will wonder why and begin to learn on their own. Once they start that, Chips, my dearest, there will be no stopping them in the whole world!" Not in the whole world! She saw through to the truth, as always. Kathie! Kathie! Kathie! Kathie! (*Overcome, steadies himself. Merrivale helps him back to his chair.*) Thank you, Merrivale. It seems that my pins are not so steady as they were. Anno domini! It was thirty-seven years ago that I brought her first to Brookfield, and we knew her for two. I am profoundly grateful for them. Few men have owned as much. Soon our first child was on the way…

The same room, 1897, daylight. Chips, 49, alone, standing at his bookshelves. Enter Kathie.

KATHIE
Wonderful news, darling Chips! The most glorious! Dr. Cole says that I am with child!

CHIPS
Darling Kathie! With child, with our child! There will be three of us soon! We will uncork the Margaux tonight! We are the king and queen of Brookfield!

KATHIE
And heir apparent! Not so apparent just yet, darling Chips, but watch out! He will be all too apparent, and soon. I will be big as a whale by Christmas, Chips, my darling, for the whole world to see, and we will have somebody new in the family by spring!

CHIPS
He or she! A new Master or Miss Chips by spring!

Projected scenes of Brookfield, summer changing to fall as Chips continues unseen.

CHIPS
You know well, good Merrivale, how happy that time can be. Champagne, cigars and celebration. We bought baby clothes, a rattle, a music box.

The drawing room again, evening, November 1897. Kathie, alone reading. Enter Chips.

CHIPS
Darling Kathie, see what I found for the baby!

KATHIE
Wonderful, Chips! (*Chips unwraps a rattle, which rattles briefly, and a music box.*) Wonderful! Both beautiful, Chips! The music box is perfect! (*Chips opens its lid to play it.*)

CHIPS
It cost six shillings at Mrs. Brool's. She marked it down from six guineas for our baby. It's older than you are, dearest Kathie, I think, and maybe older than I am.

KATHIE
Then we will honor our elders, my darling, and hold it for our child and all children to come. (*They embrace.*) It is something magic from the artisans of Elfland. We will find somewhere safe for it.

Fade out. Projections show snow falling. Fade in again to Chips and Kathie in the same room one month later. A window also shows snow falling.

KATHIE
Happy New Year's Eve, darling Chips!

CHIPS
And the happiest, happiest New Year's Eve to you, dearest Kathie! And how is our baby this evening?

KATHIE
He will certainly be an explorer. I feel him exploring his little world over and over.

CHIPS
Or she!

KATHIE
Or she!

Now projections follow Chips' account as he continues seen or unseen.

CHIPS
Then the troubles began. By spring term there were longer visits and longer faces at the doctor's. You would have been scarcely born yourself, good Merrivale, and medicine was not so far along ...

A hospital room. Kathie in bed. Chips at her side.

KATHIE
Chips, darling, it's started. They'll kick you out soon. Dr. Cole says that things are a bit touchy. Our baby has decided to stretch out the wrong way, it seems, and doesn't want to budge. Stubborn as a true Chips. Not to worry. We always get it right in the end. It will take more than a kink in the piping to stop a Chips, much less two of us! But just in case, my darling, just in case, you must know what to do. You must marry again, so that she and our baby can love you as much as I do. And you must stay just the same. You must cram your fists in your pockets when you are angry, which is never for long, and you must slide your glasses back up your nose when they slide down, which is often. And you must teach the boys, just as you have, so that they will learn to teach themselves, and teach the world, because now they are my boys too. And then one day, one wintry day at the end, when everyone is going home to bed, one drear and drizzly day far off, when all the world has jumped to someplace new, and doesn't know just where, or what comes next, when everything is falling upside down, so that our boys will have to put it right, on one such day far off, my dearest darling, I will call on you. I will knock on your door, and take your hand, and help you down the mountain one more time. And all the while, I will save a place for you, if I am sent the right way, and keep an eye on you, if their telescopes are strong enough, and put in a word for you, if I can find the right ear, because I love you forever and ever and ever. Goodbye, Mister Chips! (*Doctor and nurses move in, lead Chips out.*)

Projections show town giving way to country and then Brookfield. Chips is seen or unseen.

CHIPS
Somehow I walked the three miles back to campus in the rain. Mother and child both lost. No one there knew. I wanted to get used to things, if I could, before facing the kind words of others. (*No bitterness or irony.*) I took the fourth form as usual just before call-over,[143] setting them grammar to learn by heart as I stayed at my desk. (*A form room, boys, Chips at his desk, a window at the back showing rain.*) I was in a kind of trance, I suppose, until the hour ended and the boys filed out …

FAULKNER (last boy)
Sir, there are a lot of letters for you.

CHIPS
So there are. I hadn't noticed them. Thank you, Faulkner. (*Exit Faulkner. Chips opens and reads a letter.*) "Ludens Aprilis dolandum bone vir." (*Opens and reads the rest as he continues.*) April fool, Mr. Chipping. April fool? Of course! It's April first, 1898. Dear boys! Dolandum! Chipping! How Kathie would have laughed! Clever boys! Clever scamps! Clever Faulkner! Dolandum! Dear Kathie! How Kathie would have laughed! Dear Kathie! (*Laughing and crying together*) Dear Kathie! How Kathie would have laughed!

Fade to projections illustrating Merrivale's account. Merrivale may be seen or unseen.

MERRIVALE
I suppose I was the first to hear this straight from Chips. Now he needed rest. I asked Mrs. Wickett to keep an eye on him, and took my leave. The rest of his story is Brookfield lore, passed down from the masters and students. All agree that marriage had changed and enriched him. Anyone could see the new spring in his step, the smile, the twinkle, the confidence. Now he began to slip more humor into his lectures, little puns and ironies that make things easier to remember. When he knew that students had been coached and saw them coming, he could play that to advantage.

---

[143] Roll call

Same form room. Chips is lecturing to the same class. Faulkner, a good-hearted prankster, sits front center.

CHIPS
Thus the Senate enacted the Lex Canuleia[144], the law allowing patricians to marry plebeians. It meant that if Miss Plebs wanted to marry Mr. Patrician, and he said he couldn't, then she could say, "Yes, you …"

Chips gestures to the left, then right, then to all together, like a conductor cueing an orchestra. Faulkner leans stage left to join that group, then stage right to join the other, as those groups yell in turn:

LEFT BOYS
Can!

RIGHT BOYS
You!

ALL BOYS
Liar!"[145]

All rise to yell "Liar," and file out merrily as Chips motions them to do. Fade out. Brookfield projections as before, now about 1900. Merrivale may be seen or unseen.

MERRIVALE
Bereavement, after the first, somehow brightened and enriched him once again. It was as if Kathie had become a part of him. There was a gain in perspective, scope, dimension. He had earned the respect of the boys from that first day, and gradually their trust and admiration over more than a quarter century at Brookfield, but only now came their love. Now he had earned the right to those gentle eccentricities that so often attack parsons and schoolmasters. He wore his old gown until it was almost too tattered because Kathie had mended it once to stitch a sleeve, so he kept it. He took call-over standing on a bench by Big Hall with an air of mystic abandonment to ritual, the School List curling over a board as he read the name of each boy to repeat as they all passed by …

[144, 144] Rhymes with "Maya."

1900, Chips standing on a bench outside the door of Big Hall. Boys file in, repeating their names as he calls them. The rest, out of his sight, spoof him good-naturedly.

CHIPS
(*Calling as boys respond*) Wayne. Weaver. Webb. Wellinger. Wenn-Smith. Werner. West … (*No answer this time.*) West … (*Chips marks the list, then continues.*) … Whiteburn. Wick. Williams. Wilsey. Winters. Wise. Witt. Woodley. Worth. Wyatt. Yarrington. Yearman. Young. Zane-Willis.

All boys have now entered Big Hall. West runs in, scuffed up.

WEST
(*Evasively*) I'm sorry, sir. I took a spill at cricket and had to wash up.

CHIPS
(*Sternly, looking him straight in the eye*) Have you been fighting, West?

WEST
(*Pause.*) Yes, sir.

CHIPS
Tell me what happened.

WEST
It was about the railway strike, sir. My older brothers are both strikers. One of the neighbor boys said that the men are overpaid already. We fought.

CHIPS
Who swung first?

WEST
(*Pause.*) I did, sir.

CHIPS
Is the other boy all right?

WEST
Yes, sir. He's bigger than I am, sir, and got the best of it.

CHIPS
Do you know that what you did deserves expulsion?

WEST
Yes, sir.

CHIPS
No matter what he said?

WEST
Yes, sir.

CHIPS
Then you know never to do it again. You are on probation. You have two hundred lines.

WEST
(*Relieved*) Yes, sir. Thank you, sir. (*Runs into Big Hall.*)

CHIPS
(*To himself*) Good lad, West. The Head would rusticate him if he knew. But West has good stuff in him. One day he will be a great man, Kathie, or a damned nuisance, (*Chuckles.*) or both, as so many have been. Kathie, I think that this is what you would have done. (*Rubbing out what he had written on the list*) I think that this is what you would have done. (*Fade out.*)

MERRIVALE
(*Seen or unseen*) Sometimes the mood was somber ...

Big Hall, 1901, Chips and all 500 Brookfield students.

CHIPS
This January, it was the sad duty of Headmaster Meldrum to inform you of the passing of our beloved queen at Osborne House. It is now mine to report his own death yesterday of rheumatic fever. (*Gasps from the boys.*) The Governors have asked me to serve in his place until a successor can be found. He was the twenty-third headmaster of Brookfield since it was founded in Queen Elizabeth's time, and the only one under whom I have served since I came here to teach in 1870. His predecessor, Mr. Wetherby, who engaged me,

and who had held the office thirty years himself, died before the beginning of autumn term that year. Mr. Meldrum was a classicist, as am I, and as was Mr. Wetherby, and he thought, as do I, that the classics are taught for good cause. There is a beauty that holds. He taught that to all of us, master and student, to you and to some of your fathers. His was a life to remember, a life of renown, a guide to our journey in search of the beauty that holds.

Again projections illustrate Merrivale's narrative while he is seen or unseen.

MERRIVALE[146]
There had been talk of making Chips' position permanent, but he was not really disappointed when the Governors brought in a youngster of thirty-seven, glittering with Firsts and Blues, and with the kind of personality that could reduce Big Hall to silence with the lifting of an eyebrow. Chips was not in the running with that sort of person; he was an altogether milder and less ferocious animal. Ralston was disliked as much as Chips was loved. Efficient, ruthless, ambitious. Ralston was a live wire; a fine power transmitter, but you had to beware of him. Chips had not bothered to beware of him. Teaching was his business, and problems could be faced when met. The big row came in aught-eight, when Chips had turned sixty. He was invited to Ralston's study. Then came his urbane ultimatum:

Ralston's study, 1908.

RALSTON
Mr. Chipping, have you ever thought you would like to retire?

CHIPS
(*Startled*) No, I can't say I've thought much about it yet.

RALSTON
Well, Mr. Chipping, the suggestion is there to consider. The governors, I am sure, would agree to an adequate pension.

---

[146] The sentence beginning, "Ralston was a live wire…" is given to Rivers, in a later scene, in the novel. The two sentences after "you had to beware of him" are added. The final two quote Hilton approximately.

CHIPS
(*Flaming up*) But I don't want to retire! I don't need to consider it!

RALSTON
(*Calmly*) In that case, things are going to be a little difficult.

CHIPS
Difficult? Why difficult?

RALSTON
(*Calm as always*) Since you force me to use plain words, Mr. Chipping, you shall have them. For some time past, you haven't been pulling your weight here. Your methods of teaching are slack and old-fashioned, your personal habits are slovenly, and you ignore my instructions in a manner which I should regard in a younger man as rank insubordination.

CHIPS
(*Cramming his fists into his pockets*) But, *slovenly*, you said!

RALSTON
Yes, slovenly! Look at the gown you're wearing. It is almost too tattered to stay on your shoulders. I happen to know that that gown of yours is a subject of constant amusement throughout the school.

CHIPS
(*Fondly, to himself, as he takes his hands from his pockets to show himself the sleeve Kathie had mended*) True, very true, but it is a keepsake, rich in memory, something touched by someone in the past. (*Now looking at nothing in particular, serene, with no trace of irony, lost in thought*) And amusement of the students, kind Headmaster, can sometimes find a purpose. (*To Ralston, cramming his fists back in his pockets, indignant again*) But you also said *insubordination*!

RALSTON
No, I didn't. I said I should have regarded it so in a younger man. In your case, it's more likely a mixture of slackness and obstinacy. Take the manner in which you speak Latin, for instance. I believe I told all of the masters to follow the new style without exception. You prefer to stick to your old methods, and the result is simply chaos and inefficiency.

CHIPS
(*Defiant*) Oh, *that*! Well, I admit that I never agreed with the new way of pronouncing. Making the boys say "Kickero" at school, when they'll be saying "Cicero" for the rest of their lives, if they say it at all. And instead of "vicissim[147]," God bless my soul, you'd make them say, "We kiss 'em!" (*Laughs to himself as Ralston stares.*) Mr. Meldrum, who preceded you, spoke Latin just as I do. And so did Mr. Wetherby, who preceded him. In 1870, when he first approved my syllabus, he said, "You'll take the Cicero for the fourth." And he said "Cicero," not "Kickero"! (*Moves to the door as he finishes.*) I don't intend to resign, and you can do what you like about it! (*Exit Chips, closing the door politely.*)

Again projections trace the narrative.

MERRIVALE
Poor Ralston! He had bitten off more than he could chew. For it had chanced that a small boy had been waiting outside to see Ralston that morning. He had been listening. He told his friends. Some of these told their parents. Soon the story went everywhere. "We kiss 'em" was judged his finest touch. The whole school rallied around Chips. The Chairman of the Board of Governors, Sir John Rivers, visited Brookfield, ignored Ralston, and went directly to Chips.

Still 1908. Chips and Rivers, aged 50, alone by the Brookfield cricket oval. Cricket is played in the background, with Big Hall visible farther off.

RIVERS
Chips, old fellow, I hear you've been having the deuce of a row with Ralston. I want you to know that the governors are with you to a man. We don't like the fellow a great deal. Claims to have doubled the School's endowment by some monkeying on the Stock Exchange. I daresay he has, but a fellow like that wants watching. So if he starts chucking his weight about with you, you can tell him very politely to go to the devil. The governors don't want you to resign. Brookfield wouldn't be the same without you, and they know it. We all know it. You can stay here until you're a hundred if you feel like it. Indeed, it's our hope that you will. (*Exit Rivers.*)

---

[147] In turn, conversely.

CHIPS
(*Dabbing his eyes with a handkerchief*) Thank you very kindly, Chairman Rivers.

Kathie, you won't remember Johnny Rivers;
He came to Brookfield well before your time.
A lively soul, a Puck, a scalawag
Who hid my glasses once, so that I had
To read the Eclogues out at full arm's length
While all the class made merry.
                                        O my love,
Where have they gone, those lads, those lives, those threads
That once we wove together, you and I?
Some broken now, some frayed, but most, I think,
Woven together into something fine,

CHORUS (offstage)
Long remembered, old in story,
Lads before us come and gone.
Fare you well, lads, off to glory,
Banners high, our contest won:

We who stay will follow after,
One and all for worst and best,
Brace and beam and rail and rafter,
Each with each to stand the test,
Fellows all in tears and laughter,
Shipmates on our journey west.

CHIPS
(*Continuing as the chorus sings*)
Woven of jest and dreams, and Lord knows what,
Of cabbages and kings and poetry,
Of common things enchanted in a spell
To cast across the wind, across the world,
Across the sea and stars, wherever thought
And song and story go, then home again,
With something fine. And I will say "Well done,
Well played, my lads, well borne by each and all,

Well fought by all the school," but just for now,
I thank you, very kindly, (*Dabbing his eyes*) Chairman Rivers.

Chips dabs his eyes again. Fade out.

Act II

Scenes of Brookfield again.

CHORUS (offstage)
Long remembered, old in story,
Lads before us come and gone.
Fare you well, lads, off to glory,
Banners high, our contest won:

We who stay will follow after,
One and all for worst and best,
Brace and beam and rail and rafter,
Each with each to stand the test,
Fellows all in tears and laughter,
Shipmates on our journey west.

MERRIVALE[148]
Ralston soon went on to better things. Chips could not have known that he would meet him again, one distant day, and save his soul. The new headmaster, Chatteris, was even younger than Ralston had been, but a decent sort who let Chips carry on as before. Chips would always invite the boys the night before Christmas holidays …

Chips' drawing room, evening, December 1911. Chips and boys, including Grayson, are opening presents under a Christmas tree.

GRAYSON
(*To Chips*) Here's one for you, sir, from Australia. (*Hands Chips a Christmas-wrapped package.*)

---

[148] The third sentence here quotes Hilton.

CHIPS
Thank you, Grayson. Now off to your beds, every one of you, and off for the holidays in the morning. My best to Father Christmas, if you see him, and to all of yourselves and your families until we resume. (*The boys leave with their presents. Chips reads the card on the package.*) From Mrs. Brool! (*He unwraps the package, and takes out a letter and a second music box something like the first. He lifts the lid to play it, listens and reads the letter.*) "Dear Chips, this and the other one seem to belong to a set. Strange, that somehow I found them fourteen years and half a world apart. Perfect for your new children and grandchildren as they come along." (*The lid closes as the tune ends. Chips puts down the letter.*) Fourteen years, and no one has had the heart to tell her. Kathie, there must be beautiful music on your side. Look what dear Mrs. Brool and the artisans of Elfland have given us on this!

Fade to Merrivale, with projections of winter and snow easing gradually into spring.

MERRIVALE
I was thirteen then, and remember the winter as cold. But spring was so much the more glorious, and Chips, by all report, was still at the top of his game.

Form room, April 16, 1912. Chips and teenage boys. The window shows mid-afternoon.

CHIPS
… and Mr. Patrician said he couldn't, then Miss Plebs could say, "Yes, you …" (*Chips conducts as before.*)

LEFT BOYS
Can!

RIGHT BOYS
You!

ALL BOYS
Liar!"

All rise laughing, as before, on "Liar."

CHIPS
That concludes today's lesson. (*Boys begin to file out merrily.*) Grayson, I would like to see you for a moment. (*Grayson stays. The rest leave.*) Grayson, I don't want to be severe, because you are generally pretty good in your work, but today, you don't seem to be trying at all. Is something the matter?

GRAYSON
No, sir.

CHIPS
Well, we'll say no more about it, but I shall expect better things next time.

GRAYSON
Yes, sir. (*Walks a few paces toward the door, turns.*) Sir, (*Tearing up*) my father was on the Titanic last night. We're waiting for word.

CHIPS
Good Lord. Good Lord. Grayson, you are excused all classes today. I shall ask for prayers in chapel this evening.

GRAYSON
Thank you, sir. (*Exit Grayson. Chips goes to one knee.*)

CHIPS
Kathie, beautiful Kathie, because all the boys are your boys too, and because our little baby would have been just Grayson's age, and because you yourself lost both your parents young, and know how hard it can be to find our way alone, dear Kathie, Kathie my beauty, if you can find the right ear, please put in a word for Grayson's father.

Memories reappear as he remains kneeling. They are seen in successively different parts of the room, each in the place and light as remembered, as the real room darkens toward night. Chips' responses are to himself, face to the audience, still kneeling, as an actor mimes his part.

GRAYSON
Sir, my father was on the Titanic last night.

CHIPS
Good Lord, good Lord, Grayson!

GRAYSON
Here's one for you, sir, from Australia.

CHIPS
Thank you, Grayson ... From Mrs. Brool!

KATHIE
Chips, did you hear about dear Mrs. Brool? She is off to Australia the week after next! She has cousins in Perth, and the doctors believe that the move will be good for her. Her wonderful old curiosity shop will be closed. All Brookfield will miss her, my darling, and we most of all for her kindness to us and our baby.

CHIPS
Kathie!

KATHIE
Chips, darling, you have the gift of making them laugh in just the right places.

CHIPS
Kathie!

FAULKNER
Sir, there are a lot of letters for you.

CHIPS
Dolandum! Clever Faulkner! How Kathie would have laughed! (*Laughs and cries.*) How Kathie would have laughed!

WEST
It was about the railway strike, sir.

CHIPS
Good lad, West. Kathie, I think that this is what you would have done. I think that this is what you would have done. Kathie! Dear Kathie!

RALSTON
Mr. Chipping, I happen to know that that gown of yours is a subject of constant amusement throughout the school.

CHIPS
It is a keepsake, rich in memory, something touched by someone in the past.

RIVERS
You can stay here until you're a hundred if you feel like it. Indeed, it's our hope that you will.

CHIPS
Thank you very kindly, Chairman Rivers.

GRAYSON
Sir, my father was on the Titanic last night.

CHIPS
Kathie, Kathie my beauty, if you can find the right ear, please put in a word for Grayson's father.

Full night in the form room. The window gradually shows stars as Chips remains kneeling. Hubbub of boys' voices outside, faint at first, gradually swells.

GRAYSON
(*Offstage, shouted*) Sir! Sir!

Chips rises and turns on the electric light just before Grayson bursts in.

GRAYSON
He's all right, sir! My father was rescued! He's all right! (*Weeps with joy.*)

CHIPS
Well! I'm delighted, Grayson. A happy ending! You must be feeling pretty pleased with life!

GRAYSON
Yes, sir! (*Exit. Fade out.*)

Brookfield exterior. Projections show winter changing into spring and summer.

MERRIVALE

Chips caught bronchitis early in 1913, missed most of the winter term, and decided to retire anyhow. He was 65, and didn't want to hang on if he wasn't up to it. He retired officially at the end-of-term dinner in July …

End-of-term dinner at Big Hall, July 1913. Chips at the center of the head table, Chatteris and Rivers at his sides. Masters, students, parents, governors, dignitaries.

CHIPS[149]

(*Rising to applause*) I would like to thank Headmaster Chatteris (*Bows to him.*) for his kind introduction. Far too kind, in fact, but he comes of an exaggerating family. I remember having to thrash his father for it. (*Hushed laughter from all, including Chatteris.*) I gave him one mark for Latin translation, and he exaggerated it into a seven. (*Uproarious laughter.*) I have been at Brookfield 42 years, and I have been very happy here. It has been my life. "O mihi praeteritos referat si Iuppiter annos."[150] I need not, of course, translate. (*Uproarious laughter.*) I remember lots of changes at Brookfield. I remember the first bicycle, the first electric lights. We had a member of the staff called a lamp-boy, who did nothing but clean and trim and light lamps throughout the school. I remember Mrs. Brool, whose photograph stands in the tuck shop where she served since Headmaster Wetherby's time. She inherited money from Scotland, then opened a wonderful old curiosity shop in Ware Street, and now sends all of us old Brookfeldians Christmas gifts every year from Australia. I remember when two-thirds of the school went down with German measles, and Big Hall was turned into a hospital ward. I remember when there was a hard frost that lasted seven weeks in the winter term. There were no games, and the whole school learned to skate on the fens. Eighteen eighty-something, that was. I remember the great bonfire we had on Mafeking[151] Night. It was lit too near the pavilion, and we had to send to the fire brigade to put it out. (*Hushed laughter.*) And the firemen were having their own celebrations, and most of them (*Clears his throat.*) were in a regrettable condition. (*Uproarious laughter.*) In fact, I remember so much that I often think I should write a book. Now what should I call it?

---

[149] The second sentence about Mrs. Brool is mine.
[150] Jupiter brings back past years to me.
[151] Vowels as in "Fathering."

"Memories of Rods and Lines," eh? (*Cheers, applause and laughter.*) I remember … (*Laughter continues.*) I remember … so many things … (*Laughter dies down.*) but chiefly, I remember all your faces. I shall never forget them. I have thousands of faces in my mind, the faces of boys. If you come and see me in years to come, and I hope you will, I shall try to place those older faces of yours, but it's just possible I shan't be able to, and you will say, "The old boy doesn't remember me." (*Hushed laughter.*) But I *do* remember you, as you are *now*. That's the point. In my mind you never grow up at all. Never. Sometimes, for instance, when people talk to me about our respected Chairman of the Board of Governors, (*Bows to Rivers.*) I think, "Oh yes, a jolly little chap with hair that sticks up on top, and no idea of the difference between a gerund and a gerundive." (*Laughter from Rivers and all.*) Well, well, I mustn't go on all night. Think of me sometimes as I shall certainly think of you. "Haec olim meminisse juvabit.[152]" Again, I need not translate. (*Laughter and prolonged cheers.*)

Again, projections illustrate Merrivale's narrative while he is seen or unseen.

MERRIVALE

Chips had retired from teaching, but he kept on inviting all of the new boys to tea, just as before, at the start of the fall term. He still watched all of the big matches on Brookfield ground. He was invited to dine once a term with the Head, and once with the masters. He was elected president of the Old Boys' Club, and went to their dinners in London. He accepted an offer to edit the new Brookfeldian Dictionary[153]. He wrote articles, full of jokes and Latin quotations, for the Brookfield magazine. He could be seen in the audience at the school plays and concerts, and knew all the boys by name, as always, when they spoke to him. He was guest of honor at the end-of-term dinner, in July 1914. There was war talk. His friend Herr Staefel, who taught German, and was leaving for Germany the next morning, told him the Balkan business wouldn't come to anything. (*The photo of the assassination of Franz Ferdinand is projected, then scenes of mobilization.*) Then war. The younger masters began to volunteer. Chips was invited back. He accepted. Chatteris, who was only 37, went off to serve in '17. Once again, Chips became acting Head. It was his duty, as such, to read the list of war dead after Sunday service in Chapel …

---

[152] One day you will do well to remember this.
[153] Pronounced "Diction'ry."

1917, Chapel, boys and masters seated. Chips holds a list.

CHIPS
I'm afraid that six Brookfeldians have died this week, four in the fight for Passchendaele. That brings the total of our war dead now to three hundred twelve. Each is remembered as one of our own, and wished safe passage in his journey on. (*Looks at a list. As West, Faulkner and Grayson are mentioned, we see them as students again.*) First I must report the loss of Hadley West, class of aught-two. You will remember him as a Master of Maths and Sciences here from '12 through '16, when he enlisted. He was awarded a DSC for bravery under fire. Some of you are old enough to remember Roy Dunster, class of '12. He was one of our champion cricketers, and was cox of the Blues at Oxford. You will have read in the papers of the death of Major General Francis Faulkner, a triple first in aught-two, who wrote us all holiday greetings in Latin. David Forrester, class of '14, was one of our shortest boys, but tall in gifts and heart. He had been breveted major, in the worst of the fighting, and died at the head of his troops. Colin Grayson, also class of '14, was with us when his father was thought to be lost on the Titanic. I had not expected that it would be the father, and not the son, that I would be called to condole. Finally, I must tell you of the loss of Max Staefel, the German master, somewhere on the Western Front. The letter I received was censored, and I cannot say exactly where. He was thirty years my junior, but a close friend.

MAYNARD (one of the boys)
Western Front? Does that mean that he fought for the Germans, sir?

CHIPS
It does. He, too, was a Brookfeldian who died for his country. One day, when the war is over ... (*Air raid siren; a bomb is heard exploding in the distance.*) But not quite yet. It seems that one of our military bases nearby is being paid a call. We will be safest here. These stone walls have stood three centuries, and should shield us from anything apart from a spot-on hit. That would do for us anywhere. (*Nervous laughter from the boys. Explosions continue, still distant.*) Let us meanwhile put the time to use. It may seem to you that the business of Caesar in Gaul is of lesser concern, under present events, but that is not really the case. I have brought my copy of his Gallic Wars. Is anyone willing to construe? (*Explosion a little nearer.*)

CHORUS (*Heard from offstage as Chips and Maynard continue.*)
Alma mater, amnis pratum,
Custos nostrum es.
Cantum nostrum audi, mater,
Tibi praebitum.

MAYNARD
I will, sir.

CHIPS
Very good. (*To the boys*) Will you pass this to Maynard? Maynard, turn to page forty and read from the bottom line. (*They pass the book.*)

MAYNARD
"Genus hoc erat pugnae…" this was the kind of fight … (*Louder explosion.*) "… quo se Germani exercuerant."

CHORUS
(*Onstage students, except Maynard, join.*) Stellae dum lapsaverint, …

Very loud explosions; the room trembles. Chips holds up his hand for pause.

CHORUS (*Now offstage only*)
In perpetuum.
Recordata eris tu
Nocte dieque.

The noise abates. Chips lowers his hand.

MAYNARD
… in which these Germans busied themselves. (*Laughter from the boys, continuing as Maynard and Chips speak.*) Oh sir, that's good! (*Fainter explosion.*) One of your very best!

CHIPS
(*Very faint explosion.*) Well, you can see that these dead languages can come to life again. Eh? (*Laughter continues, softer as the boys file out.*)

Again, projections illustrate Dr. Merrivale's narrative as he moves among them seen only by the audience.

MERRIVALE
When the Armistice came in 1918, Chips was seventy. He retired again, but no more really retired than the first time, and so passed his last fifteen years. Maynard, now Member for Northcliff, and other old boys who had lived through the war would motor up to visit him at Mrs. Wickett's, and he invited the new ones to tea as always. The boys wanted to know his opinions on everything. What did he think of Lloyd George, the Chamberlain brothers? What about Churchill or Ramsey? Mussolini or Hitler? Did Germany want a new war?

Mrs. Wickett told me later on that chill November afternoon in '33, after my visit, that Chips would have two more visitors that day, and a further surprise between. The first visitor was one he could not have expected.

Chips in his drawing room. Doorbell. Chips answers it.

CHIPS
(*At the door*) Mr. Ralston, I think.

RALSTON
It is.

CHIPS
Come in, Mr. Ralston. Come in from the cold. (*Leads him in.*) I can offer you tea, or sherry, or both. How can I be of help?

RALSTON
Thank you, nothing, Mr. Chipping. I have come to ask the favor of your counsel on a personal matter. I wronged you once, and apologize. I saw even then that you have a gift that I lack. A sense of the larger context. I am in need of that now.

CHIPS
I will help if I can. (*Leads him to a chair. They sit.*)

RALSTON
You may have read of me in the financial pages. I turned from academy to investments. I had some success. The Brookfield endowment has done well with its shares in Ralston Industries, and more so when I bought them back yesterday at a price above market.

CHIPS
So I heard, Mr. Ralston, and thought there may be some mistake. I'm certain that I can persuade the directors to cancel the sale if there was.

RALSTON
Dear Mr. Chipping! There was no mistake. Tomorrow I will be arrested for grand larceny. I will plead guilty and serve 12 years in prison. The shares are worthless. I bought them back to spare Brookfield. Now Mrs. Ralston is leaving me. I am alone. If I serve the 12 years, I shall be 77 on release. There is another choice. There is also the gentleman's way.

CHIPS
I understand. Three Brookfeldians have been sentenced to prison since I came here. I visited each, and welcomed each back at the end. I'm 85 now, and cannot promise the second in your case. I tried to remind them that each day, even in prison, is a chance to build.

RALSTON
I have not built well, Mr. Chipping. The gentleman's way stops the loss. Is there a God, Mr. Chipping?

CHIPS
(*Pause for emphasis. Then, speaking gently*) There's one inside.

RALSTON
There's one inside. Yes. There is. Thank you, Mr. Chipping. Thank you profoundly. There is a chance to build. I am not a religious man, as you see, but you will be remembered in my prayers. I think I have found what I sought. If you visit me in prison, I shall be most obliged. Now I must take my leave. Thank you again, Mr. Chipping. (*Chips walks him to the door. Ralston remembers something, stops.*) Mr. Chipping, before I go, might I ask another favor?

CHIPS
I will grant it if possible.

RALSTON
Mrs. Ralston and I have applied to Brookfield for our grandson Peter. He is all we have left. He is a good lad, and quick. His father died in the Bloody Sunday troubles, before he was born, and his mother in the flu of '27. If the scandal were to ruin his chances, it would break our hearts.

CHIPS
He will be accepted. I think you can count on me, Mr. Ralston.

RALSTON
(*Weeping*) Thank you yet again, Mr. Chipping. (*Exit Ralston.*)

MERRIVALE
(*Seen or unseen*) Mrs. Wickett also told me that earlier that day, just before my own visit, she had brought him a box of his old things she had found in the attic …

Chips is opening the box in his drawing room. He takes out baby clothes, the same rattle seen before, which again rattles briefly, and then the two music boxes. He dusts the first one, reflects, dabs his eyes, and again opens the lid to play it.

CHIPS
Think of it, Kathie! We might have had a grandson, as Ralston has, just old enough for Brookfield now. Would he have shown your gift for music? Would he take to the classics? He would love the movies and airplanes and motor cars, all still strange to me in this bluff and bumptious world, and push on to stranger things because boys must. He would chase the horizon, just as we taught all the boys to do, and make us change forever to keep to the beauty that holds.

A knock on the door. Chips opens it. Enter Linford, age 12.

LINFORD
Please, sir, does Mr. Chips live here?

CHIPS
(*Amused to be called that as his real name*) I am the person you want. Now what can I do for you?

LINFORD
I was told to come here, sir.

CHIPS
(*Closing the door, leading him in*) Quite right, my boy. All the new boys are invited to tea with me. (*Leads Linford to a chair, busies himself making tea.*) What is your name, young man, and why didn't I see you with all the other new boys two months ago?

LINFORD
Linford, sir. I've been out since the beginning of the term with chicken pox.

CHIPS
Ah, that accounts for it. You know, Linford, you'll like Brookfield when you get used to it. It's not half such an awful place as you imagine. You're a bit afraid of it, yes? (*Linford nods.*) So was I when I first came here, 63 years ago. When I first went into Big Hall and saw all those boys, I don't think I've ever been so scared in my life. Not even when the Germans bombed us in the war. But it didn't last long, the scared feeling, I mean. I soon made myself at home. (*Carries the tea and cake to a table in front of Linford, sits across from him. Chips and Linford continue as he does so.*)

LINFORD
Were there a lot of other new boys that term, sir?

CHIPS
(*Laughing*) God bless my soul! I wasn't a boy at all. I was a young man of 22. And the next time you see a young man, a new Master, taking his first prep in Big Hall, just think what it feels like.

LINFORD
But if you were 22 then, sir …

CHIPS
Yes? Eh?

LINFORD
Then you must be very old now, sir.

CHIPS
(*Laughs merrily.*) Well, I'm certainly no chicken! (*Laughing*) No chicken!

LINFORD
I apologize, sir. I said that wrong.

CHIPS
Not at all, my boy, not at all. I have seen many days. May yours be as many and as happy. I'm afraid you're growing up in a very cross world, Linford. Maybe it will have got over some of its crossness by the time you're ready for it. Let's hope so, at any rate. (*The tea and cake are finished. Chips looks at his timepiece.*) I'm sorry, you can't stay. (*Chips leads Linford to the door.*) Goodbye, my boy. (*They shake hands.*)

LINFORD
Goodbye, Mr. Chips. (*Exit Linford. Chips closes the door.*)

CHIPS
Mr. Chips! (*Laughing*) Just like dear Kathie! (*Laughing and weeping together as he arrives at his chair and sits*) Dear Kathie! Good lad, Linford. Odd, though, that he said it just like that. Dear Kathie! (*Nods off, slumps to the floor.*)

Projections show photos of Great Gable, circa 1896. Chips is 48 again. He may be seen or unseen.

CHIPS
Thank you, Miss Bridges. I'm such a fool to have hurt my foot. With dark coming, and those grumpy-looking clouds, I don't know how I could have made it down without your help.

KATHIE
(*Seen or unseen*) We'll be fine, Mr. Chipping. The worst is past. Take hold of my other shoulder as we shift left here …

Now projections show Lake Windermere, still circa 1896. Chips and Kathie may be seen or unseen.

CHIPS
It seems my foot is coming round, Kathie, thanks to you. At the inn, I hobble around without my stick now.

KATHIE
Bravo, Chips! You'll be running the mile in no time! Easy does it here, though!

A different photo of Lake Windermere, days later.

KATHIE
Chips, darling!

CHIPS
Beloved Kathie!

Winter sky again. It gradually darkens into night as Kathie continues, and clouds disperse to show a field of stars.

KATHIE
Chips, darling, it's started. Just in case, you must know what to do … And then one day, when all the world is falling upside down, I will call on you. I will knock on your door, and take your hand, and help you down the mountain one more time. And all the while, I will save a place for you, if I am sent the right way, and keep an eye on you, if their telescopes are strong enough, and put in a word for you, if I can find the right ear, because I love you forever and ever and ever. Goodbye, Mr. Chips!

As she sings "Goodbye, Mr. Chips," the projection gradually fades to reveal the hospital room where Kathy died. Chips is in the bed. Merrivale attends him. Rivers, Chatteris, Mrs. Wickett, Governors, masters and Maynard, now 35, stand by. Chips rouses.

MERRIVALE
Well, you old ruffian, are you feeling all right? That was a fine shock that you gave us!

CHIPS
What has happened?

MERRIVALE
Merely that you threw a faint. Mrs. Wickett came in and found you. Lucky she did. You're all right now. Take it easy. Sleep again if you feel inclined.

CHIPS
I will soon. First I have a promise to keep. I had a visit from Ralston today.

RIVERS
From Ralston! After twenty-five years!

CHIPS
He's in a spot of trouble. He said that we'll read of it soon. He has applied to Brookfield for his grandson Peter. He was worried about the scandal. He wept. I reassured him.

RIVERS
I read[154] the financial pages, dear Chips, and I can guess what he meant. Scandals be damned! The boy will be admitted.

CHIPS
Thank you, good Chairman. Thank you all, old friends. Now I think I will catch that little nap. (*Dozes off.*)

MAYNARD
(*To Merrivale*) Odd thing, Merrivale. The new boy, Linford, who you treated for chicken pox, just told me he visited Chips this evening. He said that a lady had told him to.

MERRIVALE
A lady with golden hair.

MAYNARD
Yes! So he told me. Do you know her, Merrivale?

---

[154] Present tense; pronounced "reed."

MERRIVALE
Only by description.

MAYNARD
Poor old chap. Must have lived a lonely sort of life, all by himself.

MERRIVALE
Not always by himself. He married, you know.

MAYNARD
Oh, did he? I never knew about that.

MERRIVALE
She died in childbirth, mother and child both. 35 years ago, he told me. It was a month before I was born.

RIVERS
Pity. Pity that he never had any children. (*Linford is seen in a balcony.*)

LINFORD, MAYNARD, RIVERS AND OFFSTAGE CHORUS OF BROOKFIELD BOYS

Alma mater, amnis pratum,	Alma mater, Brookfield,
Custos nostrum es.	You are our guardian.
Cantum nostrum audi, mater,	Hear our song, Mother,
Tibi praebitum.	Offered to you.
Stellae dum lapsaverint	Until the stars fall,
In perpetuum,	Forever,
Recordata eris tu	We will remember you
Nocte dieque.	Night and day.
Usque ad diluculum,	Until the dawn,
Nunc et postea	Now and hereafter,
Elucebis denique,	You will shine forth to the last,
Hic et ubivis.	Here and everywhere.

CHIPS
(*Rousing again as the chorus begins, and continuing as they sing*) I thought I heard you, one of you, say it was a pity that I never had any children. Oh, but I have. I have. Thousands of 'em, thousands, and all boys ... (*Boys, scattered in the audience or in the aisles, repeat their names as called.*) Dunn, Dunster, ... all boys, ... Farr, Farnis, Faulkner, ... come round me now, all of you, for a last word and a joke ... Forbes-Wright, Forrester, ... My last joke, did you hear it? Did it make you laugh? Kathie, did it make you laugh? ... Gray-Choate, Grayson, ... wherever you are, give me this one last moment with you ... Wellinger, Wenn-Smith, Werner, West ... My boys.

Chips dies. Curtain.

Pupils at Desk 1870
De Luan / Alamy Stock Photo

Ann and Gordon Getty, Oil on Canvas © Alice Blackwood

AFTERWORD BY THE AUTHOR

September 21, 2023

Acknowledgements usually come in the introduction to a book. I saved them for here. My late wife comes first. She was my Jiminy Cricket whose heart and sense and instinct led us through for nearly sixty years. Lisa Delan, a first-rate poet herself, organized this project and found the illustrations. Nicolle Foland served as her worthy second-in-command. Father Paul Fitzgerald dug up the copies of the *U.S.F. Quarterly* where my poems were published some seventy years ago. Bruce Rameker, Alexandra Armantrading, Yvette Robbins, and Kristi Loder all helped with valuable advice and services.

The words "Upon a Day" begin the second stanza of "The Ballad of Poor Peter," shown on pages 41 and 42. The man we see in the cover art is Poor Peter*, but might as easily have been Chips if the children around him were all boys. The two men are much alike. Both bring the smile and the tear as well. Both are the sort to which we turn for wise advice, as does Ralston to Chips on the last day of Chips' life, while both are children themselves to the end in the sense of awe and wonderment for everything we see. My Chips and Poor Peter are not projections of myself, but of what I would like to be, and of what I would like my grandchildren to be.

Time sneaks up on us. For a few seconds, like you, I was once the youngest person in the whole world. Now I have outlived Chips by five years. I don't expect to catch up to Sir Simon, much less to Primus, but I can be grateful for a long and happy run.

*Painted by my daughter Alice Blackwood, as is the portrait of Ann and me on the facing page.

www.ingramcontent.com/pod-product-compliance
Lightning Source LLC
Chambersburg PA
CBHW051616010526
44107CB00037B/1445/J